A Chance to Dream

Heartlines

Books by Jill Young

Three Summers On
Just Matty's Luck
Valentine Night

Books by Pam Lyons

Latchkey Girl
Ms Perfect
One Of The Boys
Wish You Were Here
Girl Overboard

Books by Anita Eires

Californian Summer
If Only . . .
Teacher's Pet

Books by Mary Hooper

Love Emma XXX
Opposites Attract
Remembering Melanie

Books by Barbara Jacobs

Two Times Two

Books by Anita Davies

Always in My Dreams

Books by Vicki Tyler

Danny and the Real Me

Books by Ann de Gale

Island Encounter

Books by Anthea Cohen

Dangerous Love
Substance and Shadow

Books by David S Williams

Give Me Back My Pride
Forgive and Forget
No Time For Regrets

Books by Ann Ruffell

Friends For Keeps
Baby Face
No Place To Hide
Leaving Home
Drumbeat

Books by Lorna Read

Images
The Name is Zero
On Wheels of Love

Books by Jane Butterworth

Spotlight On Sam
Wild in The Country

Books by John Harvey

Wild Love

Books by Jane Pitt

Autumn Always Comes
Stony Limits
Rainbows For Sale
Headlines

Books by Margaret West

Home Before Dark
Search for a Stranger
Date With Danger

heartlines

Anita Davies

A Chance to Dream

A Pan Original

First published 1988 by Pan Books Ltd
Cavaye Place London SW10 9PG
© Anita Davies 1988
ISBN 0 330 30488 7

Printed and bound in Great Britain by
Richard Clay Ltd, Bungay, Suffolk

Chapter 1

I gazed out over the shimmering expanse of the lake, blue-black as ink save for the moonlight-crested wavelets. Below my sandalled feet the marble steps of the *palazzo* swept down into the silvery rippled depths where I'd swum earlier on, my suntanned arms cleaving the cool water with sure strokes. On the other side of the lake, terraced slopes of vines and olive trees were silhouetted against a violet sky where little puffs of cloud were still sunset-tinted. How could I leave all this for drizzly, dirty old London?

I felt a pair of strong hands on my shoulders, which were left bare by my flimsy silver lamé evening gown. Without turning round, I knew it was Roberto. And when, after a long pause, I did turn round, the face that stared into mine was not Roberto's but that of Frankenstein's monster.

With a hoot of crazy laughter I flung my ballpoint pen into the furthest corner of my bedroom. You're a head-case, Jacky Nelson, I told myself. Why did I always have to poke fun at my ideas like this when I was supposed to be writing a romantic story? Especially when so much was at stake. *Sweet Sixteen* magazine was offering a luxury holiday for two in the Italian Lakes as first prize for a romantic short story with that setting. There were also three second prizes of a weekend break in Scotland (I wasn't so keen on that, but I'll explain why later), and ten runner-up prizes of book tokens.

I was one of the best writers at my school. Mr Wilks, my English teacher, always praised my long, poetic descriptions. I put in lashings of adjectives and adverbs just to please him. Someone had to win that comp — so why not me? I picked up my pen and crossed out that last stupid sentence about Frankenstein. I'd just got Roberto gazing passionately into my (i.e. my heroine Louella's) eyes, when mum yelled from downstairs.

'Jacky, what are you doing up there?'

'Nothing!' I hid the writing paper inside a book on my desk. I didn't tell anyone, not even my best friend Claire, about my writing.

'Well, then, come down and help me with these cakes.'

Cakes? She couldn't be baking yet again! My little brother and sister, Paul and Cath, would grow up like Billy and Bessie Bunter if she wasn't careful. I sighed and went downstairs.

A delicious, warm smell of baking came from our cramped kitchen, where a large sponge and rows of fairy cakes cooled on a rack. An uncooked fruit tart awaited oven space. Mum, floury handed, pointed to a ball of pastry dough in a bowl.

'You can make some jam tarts from that left-over pastry if you've nothing else to do.' If only I could explain that I'd been looking forward to having time to write now that my GCSE exams were over. But she wouldn't understand.

'Are we having a party or something?' I asked. 'Or is the Lord Mayor coming to tea?'

'June and Steve are coming and anything that's left will do for the weekend,' replied mum, deftly removing the tray of golden-brown Cornish pasties from the oven and putting the tart in its place. 'June's eating for two now, so she may want to take something home with her.'

Honestly, mum's ideas on nutrition belong in The Dark Ages. And my married sister, June, isn't much better. But mum loves cooking. Since the factory closed she found the days a bit long and lonely with Paul and Cath both at school. And me, until now.

As I cut out the little tart shapes and arranged them on the baking tray, it dawned on me that mum could do this herself a lot faster. She was a pastry-cook before she married, and had kept up her skills through years of practice. She'd asked me to help because she wanted company. She missed the chatter of the other women at work.

'I didn't think you'd be spending so much time stuck in your room now you've finished studying,' she said, as though reading my thoughts.

'Just writing a few letters,' I mumbled, chucking a spoonful of jam at a tart. It missed, spattering the table with red.

'Do watch what you're doing, love. Well, I don't want to nag, but have you decided what you're going to do now? Go back to school in September, go to tech. college, get a job, or what?'

'Give me a chance, Mum. The holidays have just started. I've got ages to make up my mind.' Doodling a pattern in the jam splodge with the teaspoon, I wondered what her reaction would be if I told her the truth. That I wanted to be a novelist.

Mum sighed, taking the spoon and jam pot from me and finishing the job herself. 'So why don't you try for a few jobs now? If only you'd get out of those jeans, wash your hair and smarten yourself up a bit you'd have a good chance.'

'I don't want a job. And I don't want to make jam tarts either!' I retorted, snatching off my apron.

Without bothering to wash the jam off my hands, I ran out and slammed the front door, not wanting to stay and see the hurt look on mum's face. I couldn't explain to her what I really longed to do because it seemed so impractical – and big-headed! But all the time I was studying for my exams and keeping up with the endless coursework, I'd been looking forward to writing my own stories, to escape again into my own world of magic.

Striding down Jubilee Street, I thrust my jammy hands into my jeans pockets and wished myself back to the sunny Italian lakeside, and Roberto . . .

When I arrived home, several hours later, they'd already started tea. Paul and Cath went on cramming themselves with cake. June stared at me as though I were a half-mauled mouse that Sam had dropped on the carpet.

'Where've you been all day?' she demanded. 'Mum's had to do the baking, rush out shopping . . .'

'Don't be silly, June,' interrupted mum. 'I like popping out to the shops for a breath of fresh air.'

'But she ought to be helping you,' June insisted. 'She's at home with nothing to do now.'

Dad and Steve, June's husband, exchanged glances and carried on eating silently. Paul, who had slipped under the table, started pulling my foot. I kicked him. Not very hard, just in a joking sort of way, but he crawled out bawling that he hated me, and ran upstairs, howling.

Mum sighed and shot a reproachful glance at me. Looked like I wasn't doing too well today.

'I'll go and look after him,' said Cath in her big-sister voice. Just an excuse to leave the table and play with Paul. But Mum fell for it, of course.

'Yes, you do that, love.'

June, seven months gone and big enough to be carrying triplets, glared at me, flushed with righteous indignation, as she attacked a mega-slice of gooey coffee cake.

Her secretarial job wasn't very hard but it was full time. Knowing June, I guessed that she was putting in far too many hours at home as well, keeping her new suburban semi spick and span. It didn't do her temper much good.

'When are you stopping work?' I asked.

'Next week, and that's not a moment too soon. It's all getting too much for me now. They asked me if I wanted maternity leave so that I could go back later, but I said no thanks. Four years in that place has been quite enough.'

I was surprised. 'I thought you liked your job.'

She pulled a face. 'It's all right, but you get bored after a while. And I'm looking forward to being at home with the baby, being there when Steve comes home from work.'

She smiled at him, all lovey-dovey, and he managed a goofy grin while chomping on a chunk of fruit tart.

I decided there and then that, whatever else I wanted to do with my life, I didn't want to be like June. Barely twenty and already giving up her career from boredom. Didn't she realize that babies and housework would soon get boring too?

I didn't want to upset mum any more by starting an argument with my big sister, so I rose from the table.

'I must go now. I'm babysitting for the Parkers at half seven.'

I picked up my jacket and the folder containing my story. June eyed it curiously.

'What's that you're taking? You can't still be doing school work now you've finished your exams.'

'How do you know?' I retorted. 'I might be preparing for going back in September.'

'Well, I wish you'd make your mind up,' dad put in. 'It's up to you what you want to do, but it's time you thought about it.'

'I haven't decided yet whether to be a plumber or an engineer.'

I had the satisfaction of seeing their mouths drop open as I shut the door behind me. I grinned to myself all the way to the Parkers'. My family were so behind the times they didn't even realize that girls could do jobs like that these days!

And I hadn't let on about the contents of my folder. If only, by the end of this summer, I could achieve some sort of proof of my writing ability – get a story accepted by a magazine, or better still, a whole novel. Winning this competition would do. Then I wouldn't mind telling my family about my ambitions. They couldn't make fun of me if I'd already begun to succeed.

I began to imagine the Italian holiday. Maybe I'd meet a good-looking boy with dark, smouldering eyes like my hero, Roberto . . .

When I arrived, the Parkers were all ready to go out, with little Graham tucked up in bed. He was the same age as our Paul, but much better behaved. Or so it seemed to me, after our teatime fracas. I read him a story and he was soon fast asleep.

I settled down with my notebook to continue my tale. My beautiful and clever heroine, Louella, a Fleet Street reporter, had fallen in love with the dashing Italian count while researching some exciting mystery – I hadn't decided quite what yet, but it would probably involve the Mafia. Of course, Roberto desired her madly in return, wanted her to give up her dangerous mission and live happily ever after with him in the *palazzo* . . .

Just then the phone rang. 'Hi. It's me, Claire. How about coming shopping tomorrow?'

'Sorry, but I've spent all my money today. So I'll

only have what I earn from babysitting tonight. And I want to save that for my holiday.'

'Have you persuaded your parents to take you to Italy, then?'

'No, but I'm working on it! I'm not exactly in their good books at the moment, though. That's why I spent my money – I had to get away from it all.'

'Where did you go?'

'I took a bus out into Sherwood Forest.'

'Who with?'

I hesitated, tempted to invent a boyfriend as good-looking as her Darren, and as sweet and sensitive as Robert had been. But I decided to tell the truth instead.

'Nobody. I just went on my own. I walked around. I smelled the leaves and the grass. I watched the sunlight make spotty patterns through the trees. I saw a squirrel and lots of birds.'

'Jacky, you're a nutter! It's dangerous to wander about on your own like that. Hey, I nearly forgot. Do you fancy coming on a double date with me and Darren on Saturday? There's this friend of his you haven't met . . .'

'No thanks,' I interrupted. I remembered the last double date Claire had fixed up. The one that turned out to be a total disaster.

Chapter 2

I'll never forget that blind date with Gaz. I know Claire meant well. But although she's my best friend, we don't really have much in common. She likes to wear trendy clothes while I slouch around in my jeans.

Claire can never get further than a few pages into a book without getting bored, while I have my nose in one all the time, as my family are fond of pointing out. We don't even like the same music or drool over the same pop stars.

Yet we've been best mates all through secondary school — a sort of attraction of opposites, I suppose. She admires me for being clever and I help her with homework. I envy her good looks and easy popularity with boys. She is forever lending me her clothes and persuading me to try new make-up.

When she started going steady with Darren, the best-looking boy in the sixth, I was really impressed. No one had ever asked me out and so I pretended I wasn't too interested in boys. But when Claire asked me to make up a foursome one evening with an older friend of Darren's who went to the tech. college, a boy I'd never met, I was flattered and excited.

'You're sure to like him, Jacky,' Claire insisted.

'He looks like Brian Terry.' (That was my favourite rock idol at the time.)

'And he's a bit of a brain-box like you, so the two of you ought to get on like a house on fire.'

'Sounds great,' I replied.

Claire said she'd help me choose what to wear. In the end we decided to spend most of my savings on a black dress that made me look sophisticated. Or so I thought. Claire lent me her bright-red jacket to go over it, and she also blow-dried the ends of my long, dark hair, which usually just hangs straight down, into big curls which she pinned on top of my head, securing them with a big red bow that exactly matched the jacket. I'd never have thought of a touch like that.

As an afterthought, she also dabbed a touch of her mum's expensive French perfume, 'Desire', behind my ears.

'Wow! Can this goddess really be mousy little Jacky?' was Darren's comment when he turned up at Claire's house. His friend was going to join us at the disco.

I didn't know which of my feelings was strongest – pleasure at the compliment or resentment at being called 'mousy'. And of course I'd no idea what to reply. Well, would you? So I blushed and began to giggle, then remembered I'd made a New Year's resolution not to giggle when attractive boys spoke to me, and changed it to a scowl half-way through. The result was a rather peculiar grimace.

'But of course I recognize her usual charming smile,' Darren added, pulling a wry face at Claire and jerking his head in my direction as though I were deaf, dumb and blind.

My heart sank. It wasn't just a matter of looks, was it? Getting on with boys, I mean. I could never seem to find the right facial expression or think of anything witty to say.

'Yes, she looks smashing, doesn't she?' Claire put in hastily, trying to cover up for Darren's blunder. 'Right, are we all ready, then? Let's go.'

As we walked into the disco, a tall, good-looking boy with well-cut blond hair in a spiky style stood up and grinned at us. The spitting image of Brian Terry. And yes, this really was Darren's friend, Gaz, my date for the night. As we were introduced, I felt myself wobbling at the knees and blushing again.

'Pleased to meet you, Jacky,' said Gaz with a smile that did peculiar things to my stomach. Talk about butterflies, it felt more like a dozen sparrows flapping about in there! I was very much aware that he hadn't let go of my hand after shaking it. His hand was strong and warm in mine and I liked the feel of it as he led me towards the bar.

'What would you like to drink?'

'I'll have an orange juice, please,' I said shyly. Then I had to repeat it more loudly, because the music threatened to drown all other sound. He raised an eyebrow.

'That's what I thought you said.'

He got my orange and a pint of beer for himself. I wondered if I ought to offer to pay for mine. I believe in equality and all that, you see. But I'd spent nearly all my money on the dress and after paying to get into the disco I didn't have much left, so I just said, 'Thanks.'

I noticed my drink had a slightly different flavour from the usual orange juice, but I quite liked it. In fact, because I was desperately trying to think of something impressive to say to this hunk of my dreams, and failing utterly, I drank it quickly. And a second one that Gaz bought me as well.

I was glad when he asked me to dance. It's hard to make conversation with music blaring, even if you feel at ease with the person you're talking to, which I didn't. I kept wondering what he thought of me.

But once the throbbing rhythm got me going I stopped feeling self-conscious and began to enjoy myself. Gaz was a good dancer and we moved well together. We danced continuously through four numbers, which nearly finished us.

'Phew, I need another drink. How about you?' gasped Gaz as he led me back to a seat.

'Great idea.' The orange juice tasted even better now I was so thirsty. Soon one of my favourite records came on – one of Brian Terry's – and I jumped up to dance.

'Not again!' groaned Gaz. 'I'm shattered. Oh well, just to please you then.'

As we danced he looked even more like Brian Terry, and after a while I began to imagine it really was him. When the record came to an end I plucked up enough courage to tell him about the likeness. He grinned.

'You're not the first one to tell me that. Do you like him then?'

'I have a poster of him on the wall above my bed.'
I could have added that I used to kiss it goodnight
before going to bed, but I was too shy.

'I'm jealous,' he replied. 'I'll have to get you to put
my picture there instead.'

Just then Claire and Darren came up to us. His
arm was round her waist and she was laughing.

'Are you two going to boogie the night away, or
is there any chance of a bite to eat?' Claire asked
Gaz.

'That depends on whether Darren's ready to be
bitten and eaten yet,' he answered, winking at his
friend.

'Oh, I'm ready,' murmured Darren, holding Claire
closer and pressing his lips to her neck. Gaz slipped
his arm round my shoulder and kissed my cheek
lightly. He did it as though we'd been going steady
for a while, like Darren and Claire. Sort of casual.
But it made my heart pound.

'OK. Let's go.' Gaz, his arm still round my
shoulder, led us out into the car park. I felt confused.
Claire hadn't told me they were going on to a
restaurant. I hoped it wouldn't be too expensive.
Would Gaz mind paying for me?

And now he'd stopped at a sleek sports car and
was unlocking the door. A Porsche. I couldn't believe
it. He was only a student. How could he possibly run
a car like this?

Darren and Claire were admiring it too. From the
conversation I gathered that it belonged to Gaz's
older brother and he was just borrowing it for the
evening. The other two got in the back seat and Gaz

held open the door while I got in the front. The streets were busy with weaving lights as it was leaving-time from the pubs. Gaz concentrated on driving and I didn't want to distract him, so I turned round to talk to Claire and Darren. But they were locked in a long embrace.

Gaz turned to smile at me briefly, taking his left hand off the steering wheel for a moment to touch my thigh. It was so quick his hand was back on the wheel before I had a chance to push it away. I wasn't sure about him touching me in such a familiar way when we'd only just met. Even if he did look like Brian Terry.

We pulled up outside a block of flats and took the lift up to the fourth floor.

'You have your own flat?' I asked Gaz, really impressed.

'I share with my brother. Our parents live too far out in the country for us to get into town every day. But he's away this weekend, gone by train to London on business, so the car and the flat are ours for the time being.'

'So we could stay the night,' said Darren. Gaz smiled and nodded as though it was settled.

'I couldn't possibly stay,' I told him quickly. Claire flashed me one of her charming grins.

'Of course you can, Jacky. Just ring your mum and say you're staying at my place for the night. Then we'll ring my mum and tell her I'm staying with you. It's so simple. They'll never check up.'

That was true. My parents would never doubt me because I'd never lied to them before. But I didn't feel right about doing it now. I didn't even know if I wanted to stay all night. Though the way Gaz looked into my eyes made me feel weak at the knees, so I sank down into the deep, soft velvet settee and said nothing.

Darren grinned and winked at me, which made me blush, so I was thankful for the soft lighting. Then he hooked his arm in Claire's and steered her towards a door leading to an inner room. As it opened briefly and closed after them, I couldn't help noticing it was a bedroom.

Beyond an archway in the sumptuously furnished living-room was a brightly lit kitchen where Gaz was taking some cheese and a bottle of wine from the fridge. He cut some French bread into chunks and put it on the coffee table in front of me, with some plates and glasses. So, apparently, it was just the two of us now.

'Let's have some music,' murmured Gaz, flipping a switch as he joined me on the settee. A soft melody, 'The Nearness of You,' floated huskily into my ears. His warm hand slipped into mine, drew me closer. Closing my eyes, I felt his arms around me and his lips gently exploring mine. Not moving, hardly breathing, I wished this moment would go on for ever.

But he lifted my arms round his neck, held me tighter, parted my lips urgently with his tongue. Suddenly frightened, I pulled away. Those sparrows inside my stomach were running riot now. To cover my embarrassment, I dived for the food.

As I sank my teeth into a chunk of bread and

grabbed a wedge of cheese, Gaz said drily, 'Do help yourself.'

My insides were beginning to feel really peculiar, but I kept on munching as it saved me from having to think up anything to say. Gaz ate some too, and poured out two glasses of wine.

'Cheers.'

'I'm sorry, but I don't drink wine. Could you manage both glasses?'

He sighed. 'I daresay I could. Is there any special reason why you don't drink wine? I mean, is it some sort of religious taboo or something?'

'Of course not. It's just that I never drink alcohol. It always makes me sick.'

'Really? You're not kidding?' he sounded alarmed as he drank both glasses of wine with incredible speed. 'You mean, like – throwing up?'

I nodded, gulping down a lump of half-chewed cheese. 'But it's OK. I haven't drunk any, have I.' My words didn't seem to reassure him.

'What time do you have to be home, Jacky?'

I hesitated. I'd told mum the disco didn't finish until two-thirty and she'd said it was all right as long as I had someone reliable to take me home. But I hadn't realized we were going to leave early and go to Gaz's place. I would have preferred to continue dancing as, despite Gaz's looks, I wasn't sure if I wanted to be alone with him for long.

'I have to be in by twelve-thirty,' I lied. Rather to my surprise, Gaz made no attempt to persuade me to stay. In fact, he looked relieved. He was probably bored with me, I thought miserably. My excited mood had completely evaporated and my stomach was churning dreadfully. The cheese must have given me indigestion.

Even though the car was so quiet and smooth-running, it felt like a waltzer at the fair. As I stared through the windscreen the city lights seemed to spin before my eyes, making me sick and dizzy.

'Stop!' I cried, 'I'm going to be sick . . .'

'Can't stop here,' Gaz muttered through clenched teeth as the lights changed to green. A few yards later he turned into a quiet sidestreet and pulled up. By then it was too late. I'd finished retching – all over the beautiful dark blue upholstery of Gaz's brother's car, my smart new dress and Claire's red jacket. A sour, nauseating stench filled the small space.

'I'm sorry,' I mumbled. 'It must have been the cheese . . .'

'Not half as sorry as I am,' retorted Gaz. 'If only you'd told me earlier that alcohol made you ill I wouldn't have wasted my money on you.'

'What do you mean? I only had three orange juices.'

'Yes, but there was a double gin in each one as well.'

I groaned and started to throw up again. This time I managed to open the car door and aim it into the gutter. But I didn't feel so badly about spoiling the car now that I realized what had caused it. Of all the stupid tricks to play! I remembered how the orange had tasted different, and it was so noisy in the disco I hadn't heard what he'd said to the barman.

After that he got me home as soon as he could.

That is, he dropped me at the end of Jubilee Street, revved up and drove off again without so much as a 'goodnight'. Maybe he was afraid my parents might ask some awkward questions.

When they asked about the state I was in, I just blurted out the truth. They were shocked at his lacing my drinks, but were really sympathetic. They're great that way.

'Never mind, love,' said mum, 'I'll put the dress and jacket to soak with a bit of salt and that'll get the stains out. What a rotten thing to happen on your first date! I'm surprised that nice Claire has friends like that.'

'Well, Jacky,' dad said, 'you'd better not go on any more blind dates. Next time you make sure it's a nice boy you know and can trust.'

I didn't tell him it was the only time I'd ever been asked. He seemed to think boys were queueing up to take me out! 'There won't be a next time!' I retorted. 'I've gone right off boys.'

Chapter 3

Rain lashed the car windows. I stared out glumly at the sodden landscape as dad drove on with a resigned set to the back of his shoulders. Mum, next to him, studied the road map on her knee and tried to look cheerful. Paul had fallen asleep with his head in my lap and Cath was dozing against my shoulder.

So much for my dreams of a holiday in Italy. I'd sent off my competition story but the results wouldn't be announced for a while yet. In the meantime I'd tried to persuade mum and dad to book a holiday abroad anyway, but all my brochure-waving and pleading was wasted.

Dad hates going abroad, especially to hot places. He got sunstroke once, when we went to Spain, so that put him off for ever. All he wants, he says, is peace and quiet, fresh air, fishing, beautiful scenery and good old British food.

So here we were, on the way to Wales for two weeks. Boring! Or so I thought then, not knowing how this holiday was going to change everything, not knowing who I was going to meet ...

'If it doesn't clear, we're not going to see much of these wonderful views you promised us,' remarked mum. 'We should have listened to Jacky and gone abroad.'

'The forecast said sunny periods for Wales,' replied dad. 'Just wait until we're a bit nearer. You won't be disappointed.'

I yawned. I longed to read my book, but I couldn't move without waking up Cath and Paul and that was the last thing I wanted to do. The journey would be nice and peaceful as long as they stayed asleep.

I gazed out into the driving rain and settled down to a daydream. What if I won my Italian holiday after all? The prize was for two. I wondered who to take with me.

Claire, perhaps? She was good fun to be with and we got on well, but since the Gaz business we hadn't been as close. I didn't have a boyfriend to take. I'd hardly even thought of a boy seriously since Robert, because the Robert fiasco, coming so close after the disastrous date with Gaz, had made me despair of ever having a steady boyfriend.

I might even take mum. She loved going abroad and seeing new places like I did. But our gondola trip down the Grand Canal was interrupted by a stop for lunch.

While we ate at the pleasant little country pub, I caught sight of a handsome, dark-haired boy about my age sitting at a table nearby. Something about him reminded me of Robert, the boy I'd met in Scotland last year – that is to say, he looked like the Roberto I'd imagined in my Italian tale, so I began to weave him into my daydream.

He was with a couple who were probably his parents. Were they going on holiday too? Maybe, by one of those romantic coincidences that always happened in my stories, he was going to exactly the same resort in Wales that we were heading for. We would fall madly in love with each other, spend an idyllic two weeks together, then exchange addresses and part tearfully with declarations of everlasting love.

And when I arrived home, what did I find waiting for me on the 'Welcome' mat in the hall but a letter from *Sweet Sixteen* magazine, to say I'd won first prize for my story. So of course I immediately wrote to Rob — no, of course that wasn't his real name — inviting him to join me on the Italian trip and . . .

'Dad, she's off in the Land of Nod again!' squealed Cath, delighted to catch me out once more. She waved a hand backwards and forwards before my face while Paul began to sing, 'Beautiful dreamer, awake unto me,' in a dreadfully tuneless voice. He'd got that from dad. All this was becoming a family sport by now, which annoyed me intensely.

'Come on, get a move on, Jacky,' dad added. 'I called you three times and you didn't hear me. It's time we were on our way.'

For the rest of the journey the two little pests, refreshed after their sleep, were bouncing about, pointing out cows, sheep and horses as if they'd never seen them before, and getting me to join in the endless game of 'I Spy'. So I had no more opportunity to daydream: about Italy, the dark-haired boy in the pub, or anything else.

The hills turned into mountains that loomed up out of the mist, and at times a faint sunbeam broke through the clouds, pouring trickles of gold into rivers and lakes.

'Just look at that view!' dad exclaimed as we rounded a hairpin bend to overlook a deep and wooded valley beyond which rose a range of purple peaks.

'Bet I'll be the first to see the sea!' shouted Paul, who isn't into beautiful views. 'Look — there it is!'

'That's a lake,' scoffed Cath.

By now we'd joined a queue of cars laden with roofracks, or towing boats or caravans. Because of the narrow, winding roads it was impossible to pass. But eventually, as the late afternoon sun struggled through the grey, Paul spotted a shimmering turquoise triangle in the angle of two hillsides on the horizon.

I craned towards the window as eagerly as the two little ones now, curious to see our destination at last. Glanheli turned out to be a sleepy little village on the landward side of a cliff overlooking the sea. On top of the cliff stood an imposing white house with a bungalow in the grounds next to it. This was where our landlady, Mrs Rees, lived and the bungalow was obviously our holiday home.

We all piled out of the car to find Mrs Rees, a tall, suntanned woman in her forties, waiting to greet us with a smile. Her long, fair hair, threaded with silver at the temples, waved loosely down her back. She didn't look at all like a seaside landlady.

But it was the young man standing next to her who stole my attention immediately. His sparkling blue eyes, like the sea on a sunny day; the heart-stopping grin in a suntanned face; the slim hips and thighs in tight, faded jeans; thick, shiny brown hair that the sun had kissed with gold at forehead and temples . . .

He was the most attractive member of the opposite sex I'd ever met. All thoughts of Gaz, Robert, the boy at lunch flew out of my head for ever.

'This is my son, Glyn,' said Mrs Rees.

Chapter 4

I was delighted to find that our bungalow had three bedrooms, so I had one to myself as I do at home. Last year, in our pine lodge in Scotland, I'd had to share with Paul and Cath, which was murder as you can imagine.

Here, my white-walled room had French windows opening on to a little patch of lawn overlooking the sea. In a sunny corner was a large dressing-table that could also double for a desk. The built-in wardrobe and the single bed with its brightly patterned Welsh woven bedspread left plenty of space in the uncluttered room.

Pleased, I unpacked my things straight away, arranging them tidily in the wardrobe, the deep, solid dressing-table drawers and the bookshelf above the bed. I put my hairbrush, comb and make-up in a drawer so that I could arrange my folder full of fresh, white paper, and my fountain pen, on the dressing-table.

Then I began to scribble some rough notes for a romantic novel set in a little Welsh village on the coast. I hadn't yet thought of a title, or a name for my hero — but the latter was suntanned, with shiny brown hair and sparkling blue eyes like the sea on a sunny day.

My heroine's name was Amber, which also happened to be the colour of her eyes. I put down my pen and stared into the dressing-table mirror. My own eyes were a lightish brown, with little yellow flecks which you could only see in sunlight. By a long stretch of the imagination you might possibly call them amber. I stared at my straight, lank, dark hair, falling untidily over my shoulders, and took up my pen again.

Amber's hair was as long, black and velvety as a Welsh winter night. I didn't know if winter nights were any longer in Wales than anywhere else in Britain. I didn't suppose they were. But I thought it sounded romantic, and my English teacher always liked us to use plenty of similes. Then the mirror distracted my attention again. Over my right shoulder, where the French windows were, the sky was turning a glorious red-gold around a sun as rosy as . . . as a ripe plum. (That was another good one. I wrote it down quickly, before I could forget.)

The plum juice was staining the clouds purple and dripping red into the sea. I turned from the reflection and went out to look at the real thing. Gazing out across the little bay, I could see on the horizon the faint, shimmery outline of a castle perched on a rock that jutted out to sea. The light from the setting sun lit up the crenellated walls and towers, painting their grey a glowing red.

It reminded me of when we still had our coal fire. I used to sit and stare into the red and grey embers, seeing in them pictures of a burning city, full of tall mansions with towers and turrets and winding staircases. Sometimes I stared for so long I could see in my imagination the tiny figures of people scurrying around, fleeing the burning towers, running down spiral staircases and dashing along alleyways.

When I was little, my mum used to laugh at my dreaming up ingenious plans that could never work out. My 'castles in the air' she used to call them. It was a long time before I understood what she meant, but when I did, I started to call my daydreams 'castles in the fire', because that image was more vivid to me. I remembered the burning 'castles' at night, and how they looked in the cold grate next morning, all crumbled and smashed into grey ashes.

As I gazed at the glowing red castle over the sea, voices and the bark of a dog floated up from the beach. I edged down the little grassy bank outside the French windows until I came to a dry-stone garden wall of weathered granite. Leaning over it, I could see down to the beach below.

Two people, one male and one female, were walking along the sand with a large Alsatian. Then I realized the male figure was Glyn, Mrs Rees' son. For a moment I thought the other was his mother. She had the same tall figure, the same flowing fair hair. As they came closer I saw that it was someone much younger, a girl like myself.

Glyn picked up a stone and threw it a long way. The dog raced after it. Glyn shouted something in Welsh and the girl laughed. He took her hand and they walked on, arms swinging, past my unseen vantage point.

Of course he had a girlfriend. How could someone as attractive as he not have a girlfriend? So why this sudden sinking feeling when my spirits had been so high only a few moments ago?

Turning my gaze back to the castle on the horizon, I saw that the red glow had disappeared from its walls, leaving them pale grey and insubstantial against the darkening sky. I went back inside and sat down at the dressing-table once more. Now I knew what the title of my book was going to be. I took a fresh sheet of paper and wrote in large capitals:

CASTLES IN THE FIRE

Chapter 5

As soon as I woke I remembered where I was. The sunlight flooding in through the flimsy curtains was too bright for Jubilee Street.

I jumped out of bed and ran to the window, opening it wide. A fresh salt breeze greeted me. The wide vista over the bay was even more splendid by daylight. Running out on to the grass in my bare feet, I could see Glanheli beach, with a few boats moored at the water's edge, and the headland beyond. And farther still, shimmering on the horizon in the faint morning mist, the little castle on a rock I'd noticed last night.

Then I looked across at Mrs Rees' house and there was Glyn, grinning down at me from an upstairs window.

'Hi!' he called, waving.

I waved back then quickly ran back inside, shut the window, and peered in the dressing-table mirror. I hadn't even combed my hair. And I was in my flimsy nightie. Whatever would he think?

I dashed into the bathroom before the rest of the family woke up. Judging by the snores coming from mum and dad's room it would be some time before they'd be up and about. But the two youngsters never slept long in the mornings. I showered, washed my hair and put on some of my new talc and toilet water. Back in my bedroom, I tried the deep violet eyeshadow Claire had given me, with a light touch of eyeliner and mascara. My eyes sparkled back at me from the mirror. Claire was right. A bit of eye make-up opened up my eyes and seemed to brighten up my face.

I usually didn't bother, though. I told myself I was making an effort to look nice today to please mum and dad and because I was on holiday. I also blow-dried my hair carefully, curving it round my face, then put on my new pale-green trousers and the stripy pastel top that went with them. Makes a change from jeans, I thought.

Who was I kidding? I wanted to be sure I was looking my best just in case I bumped into Glyn again. Although I realized it didn't matter because he obviously had a girlfriend.

Humming, I went into the roomy, modern kitchen and put on the kettle. The window here looked out landwards, over rolling hills with little patchwork fields separated by dry-stone walls. Washing up could almost be a pleasure with a view like that.

I made tea, found a tray with a picture of a cat on it, and took two cups in to mum and dad.

'This is a nice surprise, love,' said mum, sitting up sleepily.

'You're a good lass,' smiled dad, rubbing his eyes. 'Give us a kiss, then.'

I kissed his rough, lean cheek and mum's soft, plump one, remembering when I was little and used to snuggle up in their bed on Sunday mornings. Paul and Cath often did that now, but this morning they were still fast asleep.

I went back to the kitchen and got myself some coffee and muesli, then decided to go for a walk on the beach before the others got up. Glanheli might not be Italy, but at least it was a sunny day and I wanted to make the most of it.

At the seaward side of the bungalow, further along the stone wall I'd found last night, was a gate, opening on to a flight of rough-hewn granite steps descending to the beach. The cliffs on either side were so tall and sheer and the stone staircase so full of twists, I couldn't see much of the beach until I reached it.

So I was surprised to see Glyn Rees, in jeans and a blue sweater that matched his eyes, walking along the sand quite near by, throwing pebbles for the dog to chase. He turned, saw me, and waved.

I waved back, then began walking in the opposite direction. I didn't want him to think I was following him. But then a pebble landed just ahead of me. The dog ran after it, barking, followed by Glyn.

'You're an early bird like me,' he said. 'So's Gelert. He needs a long walk every morning to work off his surplus energy. Would you like to come with us? We're going about five miles altogether, so I could show you where all the sights are round here.'

'Thanks, I'd love to,' I answered at once. 'But if we're going that far I'd better go back and tell mum and dad first.'

He grinned. 'Don't worry, we won't go very far. Just a rambling tour of exploration. But go and tell them, by all means.'

I flushed. He was making fun of me, as though I'd intended a double meaning in my innocent remark. His twinkling eyes, full of mischief, made me uncomfortable. As I ran back up the stone steps, it wasn't only the steepness of the climb that made my breath come faster.

Everyone was up and tucking into bacon and eggs in the kitchen when I told them I was going for a long walk with Glyn. They stared, taking in my smart clothes and newly done hair.

'That's OK, love,' said mum. 'It's nice weather, so we'll just potter about on the beach all day. Be back for lunch at one.'

'The sea air has brought colour into your cheeks already,' remarked dad, making me blush even more.

I nearly tripped on the way down to the beach again. I was so excited. It seemed too good to be true that Glyn actually wanted to show me round. But I reminded myself of the girl on the beach last night. Glyn was just being polite to his mother's guest and I mustn't start getting any other ideas.

Gelert, eager to be off, was running around in circles, barking, wagging his tail and jumping up to put his forelegs on Glyn's chest and gazing soulfully into his eyes. I knew how he felt!

'We can walk over the cliffs to the next bay,' said Glyn, 'and by then the tide should be at its lowest, so we can walk back over the wet sand round that headland over there. It's very dangerous at high tide, so don't ever try to wade or swim round it. The current's too strong even for boats.'

We walked along the beach as far as a spot where a natural pathway cut up the cliff face. Gelert went bounding up, but I had some difficulty. Glyn had to go first and show me little crevices and footholds I wouldn't have noticed. When I reached the final bit, which was very sheer, he leaned down and stretched out his brown hand to me. I took it, a little hesitantly, because it was quite a drop to the beach below, and I was afraid my weight might pull him over.

But his other hand gripped a stout blackthorn tree that grew at the cliff's edge, and he pulled me up with seeming ease. I collapsed on the short, wiry grass with a sigh of relief.

'Isn't there an easier way than this up and down from the beach?' I asked, as the steps from the garden were obviously private.

'Of course,' was his cool answer. 'But I like to make things interesting. And now you're supposed to say, "Oh, how strong you are, Glyn." '

'Do I have to?'

'It's generally compulsory for pretty young female visitors, but I'll let you off as it's your first day here.'

'If you make it compulsory, how can you be sure they're genuinely impressed?' I kept my voice light, but my heart sank at the realization that this was probably a routine he went through with many holidaymakers.

'Oh, I'm always convinced because I'm insufferably vain.' He grinned at me as I stood up. That grin I found totally irresistible even as I reflected that maybe he wasn't kidding. He *was* extremely attractive and his whole manner suggested that he was very much aware of the fact.

I shivered. Here on the cliff the sea wind was sharp, in spite of the sunshine. I wished I'd brought a woolly.

'Here, put this on,' commanded Glyn, pulling off his blue sweater to reveal a white T-shirt beneath.

'But you'll be cold without it,' I protested.

'I'm never cold. I must be thick-blooded or something.'

'Or something!'

'Feel my hand.' He took my cold one in his. It was very warm and it held on to mine far longer than was necessary for me to judge its temperature, while his blue eyes laughed into mine.

He must be flirting with me. It annoyed me to

think it was a casual game he played with all the girls he met. Or was it?

I took the sweater and pulled it over my head. 'Thanks, that's better,' I said, liking its rough warmth all the more because it had been so close to him.

In the next bay Glyn showed me where the roof of a tiny church emerged above a sandhill. Most of the rest was buried in deep drifts of sand. Further down the beach, slate and granite gravestones just showed above the sand.

'The sea used to be much further out at one time,' Glyn explained, 'but it gradually ate away the land, leaving this churchyard stranded on the beach. Twice a year a group of us dig the graves out of the sand, or they'd soon be lost for ever.'

I tried to read some of the names on the stones. They were badly eroded by the salt winds and sand, but a few remained, faintly etched.

'Megan Owen, Gwen Jones, John Evans, aged ten . . .' I read out. 'There seem to be a lot more women and children than grown men.'

'It used to be a fishing village,' said Glyn. 'Quite a few men were lost at sea and their bodies never recovered. Some people say the ghosts of the women haunt the beach on stormy nights, waiting in vain for their menfolk to return.'

I shivered again, in spite of the warm woolly, but a delicious sort of shiver this time. I like ghost stories. I began to imagine what they were like, these women.

'Megan Owen, her long dress and dark hair blowing in the wind as she gazes hopelessly out to sea . . .' I stopped, confused, as I realized I'd been thinking aloud. But Glyn didn't seem to think it was odd.

'Yes,' he said, 'I often imagine them, too. And my mother writes about that sort of thing. Historical novels, in Welsh. Rather too romantic for my taste, but they're very well researched.'

'Your mother writes novels? And she actually has them published?' I was amazed. I'd never come across an adult who wrote anything except letters to relatives and notes for the milkman. 'I like writing stories too, but I've never had one accepted.'

'Plenty of time for that,' said Glyn. 'My mother didn't start writing till after my father died. Then it was a couple of years before she had anything published. You'll have to talk to her about it some time.'

That sounded like a really good idea. Until I reflected that maybe Mrs Rees was too busy writing to bother answering silly questions from a beginner like me.

Gelert began running in circles, barking impatiently, so we set off along the beach, back towards the headland, with the big dog loping ahead, splashing in the white foam at the water's edge.

The tide had receded, leaving a long slope of wet, ribbed sand, unmarked save for Gelert's paw prints. Out in the bay a single white sail danced on the blue waves.

'I'll take my shoes off here,' said Glyn, rolling his jeans above the knee. I did the same with mine.

The sand was cool and soft under my bare feet.

But the water was very cold. I squealed as a wavelet swirled around my ankles.

'Ouch, it's freezing!'

'Run, then! That'll warm you up.' Laughing, we ran through the shallow water foaming around the rocks. They were black and jagged. I could well believe it to be a dangerous place when the high tide was beating against them.

Glyn climbed over a seaweed-covered boulder and pulled me after him into a shallow cave just high enough for us to stand upright in.

'Your little brother and sister will love playing in here. But remember, only bring them when the tide's on its way out like this. At full tide the cave's completely submerged and anyone caught here would drown. There's no way even a strong swimmer could swim out against the tide and the cliff's too sheer for most people to climb.'

'Most people? Does that include you?'

'Of course not. Years ago, when I was in the Boy Scouts, we had to climb down with ropes and crampons to rescue a dummy from that cave. But there isn't always a Boy Scout handy when you need one. Besides, Scouts these days aren't what they used to be.'

'I might have known you were a hero. Anyway, I get your point about the danger. I shan't forget.'

Looking round the little cave, it occurred to me that it would make an ideal spot for Amber, whom I mentally re-christened Megan, to be kissed for the first time by the handsome, but rather big-headed, hero. I was still wondering what to call him when I looked up to see Glyn staring at me with an amused expression.

'Do you often retreat into a little world of your own like that?'

'All the time. My family tease me about it.'

'I'm so relieved to hear that. For a moment I thought my fatal charm must be slipping away. Seriously, though, my mother's like that. It shows you must be a born writer.'

'Do you really think so . . .' I began eagerly, but then I saw his grin and realized he wasn't serious at all. Was he ever?

'We'd better be going now,' he said. 'I'd look rather silly if we were caught by the tide after my lecture to you.' He helped me back down over the rocks, which were treacherous with seaweed, then we walked back over the wet sand to Glanheli beach.

By now several people were sitting on the sand and a solitary swimmer braved the cold sea. In the distance I could see mum and dad sitting in deck chairs with Paul and Cath playing in the sand nearby.

'Do you want to join your family now or come along a bit further with Gelert and me?'

'I don't mind going further,' I replied, unable to resist a coy sideways glance at him as I said it. He noticed and laughed.

We climbed up the easy way from the beach this time, with Gelert sniffing at our heels. Then along the cliff road, past our bungalow. A couple of miles further on, the cliff rose even higher, its edge clothed with a dense thicket of pine trees, gorse and furze, and beyond them, the sea.

'There's a village down there,' Glyn pointed it out. 'It's called Nant Garregog.'

I looked. 'I can't see anything but trees and bushes. How do you get to it?'

Glyn showed me a little stony path like a sheep track leading down from the main road. It wound down behind a clump of trees and disappeared.

'Down there's the only way. It's an hour's walk, at least – and double that time to come back up. Outlaws and rebels used to hide out there in the old days because it's so hard to find. Not even a horse or donkey can get down there, only an active person on foot. Anything they couldn't carry on their backs had to be brought by sea. There's a lovely beach there, almost always deserted, even on bank holidays. No one bothers going to a place that's so hard to find.'

'Don't the village people themselves use it?' I asked, surprised. He laughed.

'It's over fifty years since the last inhabitant moved out. It's a ghost village now, the houses are all derelict. Maybe I'll take you down there some time. We could take a picnic lunch and spend the whole day there.'

'Oh, yes, I'd love that,' I said, imagining the two of us on a deserted beach together all day. 'But wouldn't your girlfriend object?'

He looked surprised. 'Moira? I shouldn't think she'd mind my taking you and your family out for a day. She'd probably come with us.' Then he grinned, as if a sudden thought had struck him. 'You didn't think I meant just the two of us, did you?'

'Of course not!' Blushing furiously, I bent down to pat Gelert to try to hide my confusion. 'I just thought . . . I thought she might object to tagging along with us instead of being alone with you.'

He shrugged, shaking his head. 'We've been going steady for years. We have plenty of opportunity to be alone together.'

A surge of intense jealousy replaced my confusion.

'Anyway, why isn't she with you now?' I demanded.

He smiled indulgently. 'Moira's a very late riser, unlike you and me. In fact, she's rarely up and about much before lunchtime.' He glanced at his watch. 'Which reminds me — we'd better be getting back. My mother's expecting me for lunch and then I have a date with Moira.'

So this morning with me was just to fill in the time while Moira slept.

Chapter 6

I wasn't very good company that afternoon. I mooched around on the beach, snapping at Paul and Cath, and flatly refused to help them build a fort to hold back the tide. In the end I decided to go for a swim, even though it wasn't too warm.

I'm a strong swimmer. At home, if I was in a bad

mood – which was quite frequently! – I used to go to the local swimming baths and just swim backwards and forwards the length of the pool until I was tired out and my bad mood had evaporated. Sometimes I did as many as sixty or seventy lengths in that way, so I soon improved my speed and stamina.

I prefer swimming in the sea, even though it's colder. Salt smells and tastes pleasanter than chlorine, and you can look around at the scenery while you're swimming. Also, you don't keep bumping into other swimmers.

Today I was annoyed with myself for beginning to weave romantic daydreams about a boy I knew could never be mine. But no matter how much I told myself not to, I couldn't help thinking about Glyn and wondering what he and Moira were doing. I kept remembering my glimpse of her on the beach last night, trying to picture what she looked like close to. I supposed she must be very beautiful, because a boy like Glyn could choose anyone he liked. I remembered how I'd made a fool of myself by imagining he was inviting me to spend a day alone with him, and felt hot with anger at myself. I'd tried to cover it up, but he wasn't fooled.

So I swam as hard and fast as I could, trying to work all the bad temper out of my system. I made my way out to sea, looking around at some of the landmarks on shore that Glyn had pointed out to me in the morning. No one else was swimming now. I liked the feeling of being the only one out in the little bay. It gave me a sense of freedom.

I didn't stop until I felt tired. Then I turned round

and looked shoreward. To my surprise I was a very long way out. The people on the beach looked like tiny coloured dots. I tried to make out which tiny coloured dots were mum, dad, Paul and Cath, and eventually succeeded in placing them because I could see the bungalow on the cliff just above where they should be. I thought mum and dad were on their feet, waving, but I couldn't be sure.

I hoped they were. I felt like having someone to worry about me. That sounds really selfish, doesn't it? But I'm like that when I'm in a bad mood. I began to swim back very slowly and listlessly, with frequent stops to tread water or float on my back for a rest.

The distance between me and the shore didn't seem to be getting any less. On the cliff, a little way along from the Rees' white house, I could make out a figure standing with a dog. Could it be Glyn? Maybe he hadn't gone out with Moira after all. Maybe she was still in bed. Or perhaps he'd decided he preferred to be with me after all. Or what if some sixth sense had told him I was in danger and he'd come to rescue me?

I liked that last scenario best of all. As I plodded on half-heartedly towards the shore, I imagined Glyn borrowing a speed boat and dashing out here to fetch me safely back to shore. The thought of not having to bother making the wearisome swim all the way made my limbs feel like lead. I stopped to rest more and more often.

Fixing my gaze on the figure on the cliff, I saw it move, making its way along the cliff towards the hard way down to the beach, followed by the dog.

It wasn't easy to follow its progress down the beach towards the water in the midst of all the other coloured dots. But the four-legged figure at its heels helped me keep track of it.

I saw the figure push a boat off the shore and jump in, followed by the dog. It was a rowing boat, slower and less dramatic than the flashy speed boat of my imagination, but very welcome nevertheless. I could see Glyn's distant figure straining at the oars, with Gelert sitting up in the stern.

I rested a while, watching it draw nearer very gradually, then began swimming towards it. As it came closer I saw that the dog was not Gelert, but a black-and-white Welsh sheepdog. And the rower was not Glyn but a stranger, a much older man. He smiled and waved as the boat drew level with me.

'Hallo there! Bit far out, aren't you? Are you all right?'

I was so disappointed at its not being Glyn after all, I shouted back, 'Yes, perfectly all right, thank you!'

And began swimming towards the shore as if I really meant it. I put my face down and did the crawl properly, drawing breath only every four strokes, my arms propelling my body cleanly through the water like a paddle steamer. Anger with my stupid imagination gave my limbs energy once more, and when I finally paused to look up I had covered several hundred yards. The shore was definitely a lot nearer now. I set off again at a good pace.

Why hadn't I told the man in the rowing boat that I was tired and asked him nicely to take me back to the beach? I'm sure he would have obliged. It was a sort of stubborn pride, I suppose. When I have caught myself in a particularly silly daydream, I react by being very tough with myself. So I reckoned now that if I had got myself out here all because of bad temper over a boy I shouldn't have been mooning about anyway, then I could get myself back again under my own steam.

And in the end I did. But when I flung myself down on the sand next to my family I was absolutely exhausted.

'You were so far out we couldn't see you,' Cath accused.

'We thought you'd gone and drownded,' added Paul.

'Perhaps you shouldn't go quite so far on your own, dear,' suggested mum. I turned to dad for his reaction – but he was asleep with a newspaper over his face.

As I started to rub myself dry, Cath said: 'Glyn was here, wasn't he, Mummy. And Moira. They're nice. They helped us build the fort.'

I was wishing I could have seen Moira properly, when mum looked up from her magazine. 'Oh, yes, love. I forgot to tell you. Glyn came to give us his mother's invitation to dinner tonight. Wasn't that nice of her?'

'Yes, I was looking forward to having a long talk with her. Glyn says she's an author.'

'Oh, well – that explains why she doesn't keep guests in that big house of hers. Wants peace and quiet, I expect. It's got five bedrooms, you know, and there's only her and Glyn. What a waste! I was wondering why she didn't do bed-and-breakfast as well as letting the bungalow.'

I could imagine mum really enjoying doing something like that. 'You'd like to have a big house and be a seaside landlady, wouldn't you Mum?'

She sniffed. 'Don't you start! Dad's already suggested buying a house here. It's all right for him to talk. I'm the one who'd be doing all the work. What would he do?'

'Fishing . . .' came a little murmur from beneath the newspaper. Mum sniffed again.

Before they could start an argument, it was time to gather up our things and get back to the bungalow to get washed and changed. Mum impressed on Paul and Cath that they had to be on their best behaviour if they wanted to stay up late at Mrs Rees'. I wondered if Glyn and Moira would be there too. I was curious to see what sort of girl she was, yet I hated the thought of seeing the two of them together. I wondered if I might have the opportunity to discuss my writing with Glyn's mother.

I took along a folder containing some of my old stories, including a copy of the one I'd sent in for the competition, just in case.

Chapter 7

A strong smell of burning greeted us in the hallway.
Mrs Rees appeared, looking rather flustered, but with
a warm, welcoming smile.

'Do come in! Sit down and make yourselves at
home. I've just burned the potatoes, but we can have
some boiled rice with it instead. Shan't be long.'

With that she dived back into the kitchen, leaving
us to seat ourselves in the spacious, elegant dining
room which had a glorious view of the sea. After
giving Paul and Cath orders to sit still and not fidget,
mum pulled a funny face at me.

'Burnt potatoes – and probably hairs in the soup!'
she whispered with a giggle. This was obviously a
reference to Mrs Rees' long, flowing hair. I just glared
back at mum and said nothing. Just because she was
a first-class cook and housekeeper she seemed to
think all women should be the same.

Apparently Glyn was not going to be present. I
didn't know whether to be relieved or sorry.

Soon Mrs Rees entered, carrying a steaming
casserole, and I jumped up to help by fetching the
dish of rice. It turned out to be some French recipe
which I thought was very tasty, but Paul and Cath

left quite a lot behind on their plates, then made pigs of themselves with strawberries and ice-cream.

'And where's your son this evening?' Mum voiced the question I'd been longing to ask.

'Oh, he's borrowed my car to take his girlfriend to the cinema in Caernarvon. It's about thirty miles, so they'll probably be late back.'

'Caernarvon — oh, yes! That's where we want to go to see the castle . . .'

The rest of the talk flowed over my head as I imagined what it would be like if I were Glyn's regular girl and he'd taken me instead. The castle I'd seen on the horizon must be Caernarvon Castle, I thought, and that reminded me of *Castles in the Fire*. I decided to make it a historical novel, set in a nineteenth-century Welsh fishing village. I would have two main female characters in it: a poor fisherman's daughter whose father had drowned at sea, and a beautiful, aristocratic girl called Amber. The latter's hair was changed from black to blonde, and now it was Megan who had the jet-black, velvety hair. My handsome hero was madly in love with Amber and hardly noticed poor little Megan, but I knew the latter would win his heart in the end . . .

'Jacky, JACKY! Don't you hear Mrs Rees talking to you?' Mum's voice broke into my musings. Paul and Cath giggled delightedly.

'Beautiful dreamer . . .' they began to chorus, but dad told them to shut up. Ann Rees offered them some more ice-cream, which they accepted at once. She smiled at me sympathetically.

'Don't worry, Jacky. I'm very absentminded

myself. I was just asking if you were in the sixth form at school.'

'Not yet. That is, I don't know if I'm going back to school in September or getting a job. I guess I'll wait and see what my GCSE results are.'

'Good idea. You've plenty of time to make your mind up. Enjoy the summer first. But have you any idea what you'd really like to do?'

I hesitated, then shook my head. I longed to tell her about my writing, but not now. Not in front of mum and dad, and especially not in front of Paul and Cath.

'That's the trouble,' said dad. 'She seems to have no idea. Won't even discuss it with us. Does Glyn know what he wants to do?'

'Oh, yes. He's always wanted to be a vet. It's a very long training, but he's quite determined. He's always loved animals.'

I imagined those strong, suntanned hands of his holding a sick kitten, firmly, yet kindly. Stroking it, telling it not to be frightened. I was just beginning to imagine myself as the kitten, when Paul started to cry, saying Cath had pinched him. Both their faces were glowing pink from the day's sun.

'They're tired, poor things,' said Mrs Rees.

'I'll take them back to the bungalow and put them to bed,' I said, 'so you two needn't rush back.'

'That's sweet of you, dear,' said mum. 'Off you go then, kids. Dad and I will come and say goodnight later.'

'Goodnight,' said Mrs Rees. 'And don't forget about the disco tomorrow night.'

'What disco?'

'Didn't Glyn invite you to go with him this afternoon?'

'She was swimming and I forgot to mention it later,' said mum. 'I'll tell you all about it when we get home, Jacky. You go and put the little ones to bed now.'

I could understand her reluctance to delay me any longer, as Paul's crying was building up to a crescendo and Cath had begun to whimper in sympathy. But I was puzzled as to why Glyn had apparently invited me to a disco. With Moira, presumably. Was it his mother's idea, like the meal tonight, I wondered as I took Paul and Cath firmly in each hand and led them across to the bungalow.

When they were settled in bed, I told them a story about smugglers on the Welsh coast, which I made up as I went along. I was just getting to the most exciting bit (at least, I thought it was) when I realized they'd both fallen asleep! So much for the dramatic suspense in my storytelling.

Retreating to my own room, I began to write the new version of *Castles* I'd dreamed up earlier on, but found myself writing 'Glyn' instead of my hero's name. Whatever was I thinking of?

A couple of hours later, the sound of a car drew me to the window. The Rees' dark blue estate had stopped outside the tall white house next door. But no one got out.

Unable to tear myself away, I stood there watching and waiting for five, ten, fifteen minutes. No use telling myself how stupidly I was behaving, standing here like a dummy, imagining Glyn kissing Moira inside that car. It was none of my business, it was pointless to think of Glyn, but I longed to see what Moira was really like.

At last Glyn stepped out, followed by the tall, fair-haired girl I'd seen on the beach. She was closer to me now, and under the porch light I could see that she was tanned and shapely in her figure-hugging white dress. I could never look like that in a million years.

Stepping back quickly, I heard the front door close behind them. Stop mooning over a boy who belongs to someone else, I told myself sternly, going back to my writing. But I just sat there chewing my pen until I heard my parents at the door. So, what did mum have to tell me about this disco?

Chapter 8

But mum seemed reluctant to say anything much.

'Oh, apparently there's a new club with a disco for youngsters opening in the village. Everyone's been invited free for the first night and Glyn thought you might like to go, that's all.'

'But, Mum, did he ask me to go *with him*? Because that's how Mrs Rees put it.'

'I've told you more or less what he said, love. I can't remember the exact words.'

'Oh, Mum! The exact words are so important. Don't you understand?'

Dad raised his eyebrows in amusement. 'Like that, is it? Do you fancy young Glyn, then?' He's really quick on the uptake, my dad. Mum gave him a warning look. I couldn't imagine why.

'It's time you were in bed, Jacky,' she said. 'I'll pop in and say goodnight in a minute.'

I stared at her in surprise. It was a couple of years at least since she'd told me what time to go to bed. And I generally said goodnight to both of them before I went. So I could only assume that this was mum's not-too-subtle code for 'I've got something to say to you alone'.

Sure enough, I hadn't been in bed very long when she bustled in, looking as if she wasn't quite sure how to begin.

'I didn't want to say too much in front of your dad,' she said, 'because you know what he's like for teasing you, and sometimes you take life far too seriously. You ought to relax a bit, enjoy yourself and have a bit of fun like June used to at your age.'

'Is this a general discussion on philosophy, or do you have something to say about Glyn?'

'Now stop trying to be clever, young madam, and listen. That young man brought his girlfriend in to meet us tonight. They've been going out together for two years and a very pretty, well-mannered girl she is too. Just home on holiday from boarding school. Now, tomorrow she's off to see some friends of hers

52

from school and staying with them for a week. So naturally, when Glyn says he'd like you to go with him to the disco tomorrow night . . .'

'He's only asking me because he's at a loose end, and I happen to be available,' I finished off for her. 'Really, Mum, I'm quite capable of working that out for myself, you know. This morning he took me for a walk because Moira always sleeps late. I'm not getting any daft ideas about him.'

'I'm glad you understand, love. Only after that business with Robert in Scotland I couldn't help being a bit worried. You have such romantic dreams, and they're so often quite unrealistic. You have to realize that life just isn't romantic, unfortunately.' She stared at me hard, trying to make out if I really meant it, about not getting daft ideas. I smiled, or tried to, but all of a sudden my lips began to quiver.

She put her arm round my shoulders and gave me a squeeze.

'Oh, cheer up, Jacky! It's not the end of the world. One day you'll meet someone you like much more than Glyn and you'll wonder what you ever saw in him. I must admit he's a very good-looking young man, but I think he fancies himself too much. It'll be nice for you to have a companion for part of your holiday, as long as you don't read any more than that into it.'

'I know all that, Mum. And it's not going to be like it was with Robert. I'm a year older and wiser now, don't forget.'

We said goodnight and I turned over as if to sleep. But I knew I wouldn't. Mum hadn't told me anything

I didn't already know. But what hurt was that she had seen through my feelings so easily. So it must follow that everyone else could too. Even dad. And another thing that hurt was the way she'd described Moira to me, not knowing I'd already seen her.

She was really saying that Moira was so much more attractive than me in every way, it would be quite impossible for me to dream of competing with her. I'd worked that out before, but it still hurt to find that mum thought me unattractive. I wondered if dad thought the same.

They'd both had such a bad time with me over Robert, I couldn't blame them for being a bit wary of going through it all again, I supposed. But I don't really think I make the same mistakes twice. What attracted me to Robert was that he was so completely different from Gaz. I mean, it was obvious that if I hadn't happened to be allergic to alcohol, Gaz's idea of a first date would have been to make mad, passionate love on the settee and maybe even get me to stay all night. But Robert wasn't like that at all. He was a serious type of boy, quite naive in some ways, and the same age as myself.

He loved the countryside and natural history, and we'd been on some long rambles together around the lochs and hills. He was even more romantic than I. He told me several times that he was in love with me, and that I was the nicest person he'd ever met. But he never tried to kiss me or even put his arm round me or anything like that. I thought that showed he was really sincere and respected me.

I can laugh at this now, but at the time I thought

it was the most wonderful thing that had ever happened to me. We went into this souvenir giftshop in the village near where we were staying, and he bought me a ring with some coloured glass in it. He put it on the third finger of my left hand, then said, 'We're engaged now, Jacky. But we'd better not tell our parents because they'll think we're too young.' So he bought a chain as well, imitation silver like the ring, so that I could wear the ring round my neck all the time, under my clothes where nobody could see it. I didn't care about it being only a cheap ring. He was so good looking and so serious and seemed to like me so much.

When the two weeks came to an end we promised to write to each other every week, and never to go out with anyone else. I said I'd always wear the ring round my neck, even under my school blouse. And I promised to persuade my parents to invite him to stay at our house later on, then he would ask his parents to invite me back.

When two weeks went by without my receiving a reply to my first letter, I asked dad if I could phone him. He said, 'All right, but don't stay on too long as it's long distance.'

It turned out that Robert didn't want to talk for more than five minutes, because I'd interrupted one of his favourite TV programmes. But we talked long enough for me to find out that he hadn't received my letter. It must have got lost in the post, I thought. So I wrote him another. But he didn't answer that one either.

And whenever I phoned, his mum or dad said he

was out. This went on for weeks, and I kept sending more letters, asking him why he didn't get in touch with me. I got terribly upset over it. I refused to go out except to school, stopped eating and became very thin. I spent hours lying on my bed, crying. Mum took me to the doctor, who prescribed some tablets, but they didn't do much good, except make me feel sleepy a lot of the time so I tended to fall asleep on my bed instead of crying.

In the end my dad phoned Robert's parents and explained the situation to them. He said they must get Robert to ring me himself and tell me not to write or phone any more. So he did. His voice was very quiet and sounded frightened.

'Hello, Jacky. It's me, Robert.'

'Everybody says you don't want to talk to me. Is that true?'

A long pause. 'Well, you see, I've fallen in love with another girl. I'm very sorry.'

'Have you got engaged to her?'

'Er – yes. But we haven't told our parents yet. They'll say we're too young.'

'I see. Well, goodbye then.'

'Goodbye.'

I put the phone down and pictured this other girl wearing a ring round her neck under her school blouse. Suddenly I saw the funny side of it. I laughed and laughed until my sides ached.

Mum and dad stared at me in alarm. They thought I'd gone crackers, until they realized I'd finally got Robert out of my system. After that I began eating and behaving normally again and never mentioned Robert.

So I could understand why mum was now so concerned about my feelings for Glyn. But Glyn wasn't anything like Robert. He'd had the same girl-friend for two years and wasn't likely to finish with her just because I'd come along. I had enough sense to know that.

I did wonder, though, as I drifted off to sleep, why Moira had decided to go off to her friends for a week when she could be with them all term at school. And why, knowing that she was going away tomorrow, she hadn't made the effort to get up early for once so that she could spend the whole day with Glyn. Maybe she was used to having good-looking boys in love with her and took him for granted. Maybe he'd get tired of her attitude. Maybe . . .

Once more I couldn't resist building a romantic daydream involving Glyn and Moira breaking up and Glyn and I getting together. Then it turned into a proper dream as I fell asleep.

Chapter 9

'Jacky, Jacky! It's pouring with rain and we're all going on a day visit to the holiday camp!'

Cathy's excited squeal pulled me abruptly back to

consciousness. I pulled the blankets over my head and mumbled, 'You won't catch ME going to a holiday camp!'

About to doze off again, I suddenly remembered that today was special. Glyn was taking me to a disco! What on earth would I wear? I had all day to think about it, but the excitement made me feel wide awake.

'Are you sure you'll be OK on your own all day, love?' asked mum at breakfast-time. 'The forecast says it isn't going to get any better, so you can't go on the beach.'

'Oh, I'll be all right. I'll just stay here and read, maybe write a few postcards.'

The last thing I wanted to do, especially after mum's lecture last night, was to give the impression that I was mooning over Glyn. Even if I was.

As soon as they'd all gone, I went to my room to carry on with *Castles in the Fire*. My heroine was going to meet the hero at a masked ball at the manor house. In her borrowed finery, no one would recognize her as a poor fisher-girl . . .

When I stopped, I found to my surprise it was eleven-thirty. Gazing through the window at the white house next door, I wondered if Ann Rees was writing too, or if she did her housework in the mornings. What would it be like to have nothing to do but write all day? Sometimes I thought it must be heaven on earth to shut yourself away in a make-believe world where no one would disturb you for hours on end. At other times I thought it must be lonely.

Then it occurred to me that this would be an ideal opportunity to go and see Ann to discuss my writing ambitions, without any of my family knowing. Glyn had told them yesterday that he was going out fishing all day, so there was no danger of appearing to chase after him.

Collecting my folder of old stories from the bottom of my suitcase, I threw a mac over my shoulders and ran through the rain.

'Hello, Jacky, this is a nice surprise! I thought you'd gone out with your family.'

'No. I hate amusement arcades and funfairs. I was hoping, if you're not too busy, that you might look at some stories I've written. I've never shown them to anyone else before.'

'Why, yes, of course. Glyn told me you did some writing. Come in and have a coffee while we chat.'

Sitting in the large, homely kitchen, I watched her – tall in a brightly printed, loose kaftan – set the coffee machine bubbling and take a chocolate cake from a tin.

'You're as bad as my mum,' I said. 'Trying to make everyone fat.'

'Oh, I'm sure my cooking can't compete with your mum's. She used to be a professional, after all.' Seems like my parents told her their life stories after I left last night.

'Bring your coffee and cake through to the study and I'll show you some of my books.'

Seated in the cosy, untidy, book-lined room, I gazed with admiration at the two whole shelves containing the novels she'd written – hardbacks and paperbacks — and flipped through one of them while she looked at my folder.

She read one story right through, frowning with concentration, then flicked through the rest, pausing now and again at a passage that caught her eye, sweeping aside her long, flaxen hair in an absent-minded gesture.

I bit my lip nervously. This was the first time I'd shown my work to anyone and the suspense was agonizing. Would she think my ambitions were childish nonsense?

At last she looked up and smiled. 'Well, Jacky, it's obvious that you love writing and have a great talent for it, but from a professional point of view these stories have several faults.'

'Oh, I'm sure they have. I was hoping you could tell me what they are.'

'To begin with, the style. You have too many adjectives and adverbs, too much description of people and places. Too many elaborate metaphors and similes.'

I was very surprised to hear that. 'But Mr Wilks, my English teacher, likes those. He says my style is poetic!'

She smiled. 'I'm sure he does. Teachers of literature read books in order to admire the artistic skills of the writer, but ordinary people like you and me read to find out what the characters do and think and feel.'

I thought that over. I remembered the books and stories that I'd enjoyed reading most, and realized she was right.

'There's something else, Jacky. Your stories all

seem to be set in exotic, faraway places. The characters are all very rich, very beautiful and very successful.'

'That's because I like to daydream about being like that!'

'Exactly. It's called wish-fulfilment, and often the readers enjoy it as well. But mostly they want to read about characters more like themselves. Next time, try writing about what you've actually experienced.'

I nodded. 'That's something Mr Wilks has told me, too. I'm glad you and he agree on something!'

Thanking her for the coffee and cake, and the advice, I was about to leave when a thought struck me.

'Oh, by the way – please don't mention this to my family. They musn't know anything about my writing or they'd tease me to death!'

She raised an eyebrow. 'Really? Well, I won't mention it, if you want to keep it a secret.'

'Thanks. Maybe I could come round again some time?'

She smiled and nodded. 'Goodbye for now!'

As I walked back to the bungalow the clouds parted and a shaft of sunshine lit up the cliff edge and the sea. The rain had stopped. The still-wet grass shimmered in the noonday light. A good omen for this evening, perhaps?

Chapter 10

Glyn arrived five minutes early. But I'd spent so long choosing what to wear, then changing my mind, doing and re-doing my hair in what I hoped was a sophisticated style, that by the time he came, Paul and Cath were almost as excited as I was.

'I want to come too!' yelled Cath, jumping up and down. 'Glyn, can I come too? I want to put on my best dress and mum's scent like Jacky and come with you.'

'This isn't my best dress,' I hissed at her. 'It's only stuff I wear for the beach. And it's your bedtime.'

Glyn grinned at me and winked at Cath. 'She can come if she likes, you know. I'd be delighted to have two pretty girls to dance with. Your parents can come too. I don't mind.'

I flushed, thinking he must be making fun of my nosy family. And I couldn't help noticing the way he was being charming and flirtatious to Cath and my mum. He was obviously the sort of boy who's like that with all members of the opposite sex, no matter what their ages. So when he was being nice to me it didn't mean a thing.

As I got into the car, I noticed Gelert sitting up in the back seat, panting with his tongue lolling out, the way dogs do. His expression looked disconcertingly like a grin.

'Do you always bring your dog out on dates?' I asked.

'Of course. He protects me from the advances of girls who go wild with lust for me.'

'And I expect there must be lots of those, as you're so irresistible.'

'Naturally. He earns his keep, does that dog. Don't you, Gelert, boy?'

The big dog woofed agreement and began to nuzzle the back of my neck. I sat up very straight and leaned forward a little. I usually like dogs, but I'd spent ages putting my hair up in curls, and I didn't want him to spoil it.

'You look fantastic tonight,' remarked Glyn, as though reading my thoughts. 'You certainly seem to have caught a lot of sun in one day.'

I glanced at him sideways to see if he was pulling my leg again, but his face was serious, his eyes gazing steadily at the road ahead. The reason I thought he might be joking was that my suntan had come out of a bottle. And a gravy-browning bottle at that!

Feeling conscious of my paleness compared to Moira and the other locals, I'd trekked to the village shop in vain that afternoon: they didn't sell fake tan. So I'd used some browning from the kitchen cupboard instead. A few dabs of mum's romantic perfume had disguised the slight meaty aroma.

But as Gelert sniffed and began licking the back of my neck again, I realized he wasn't fooled. That scent of gravy spelt instant appeal to his doggy senses.

Squirming out of his reach, I turned round to pat his head. He tried to nuzzle me again.

'I think he fancies you, Jacky.'

'Yes, for supper!' And you don't know how true that is, I said to myself. For the rest of the way I managed to stay out of reach of the dog's probing tongue by perching uncomfortably on the edge of my seat. Fortunately, we didn't have far to go.

The disco was in a large, freshly decorated room in a trendy new hotel. As we walked in, I realized Glyn hadn't been kidding about taking mum and Cath. As well as masses of people our age, there were grannies and grandads, not to mention parents! And even babes-in-arms and a few toddlers. The sound of their chatter competing with the loud disco music was deafening. And the chatter was all in Welsh so I couldn't understand a word.

Glyn grinned at my surprise. 'It's because it's a free opening night,' he explained. 'It's a sort of local tradition. Anyone can come.'

Even me, I thought. And all my family. Glyn hadn't intended it to be just the two of us after all. It was a jolly village free-for-all, and here was I with my hair pinned up, all dressed up like − like a dog's dinner, I reflected, eyeing Gelert, who was now sniffing enthusiastically round my bare legs.

Everyone was dancing, in a variety of weird and wonderful styles. The floor was packed. One woman was actually trying to dance while holding a baby in her arms! Most of the teenagers were in jeans and T-shirts, like Glyn.

Even in my red sundress I felt overdressed. I shuddered to think how out of place I'd have looked in the black and silver dress I'd almost worn.

We joined in the dancing. It was so crowded we all kept bumping into each other, but nobody seemed to mind. Glyn and his friends talked and teased each other as they danced. Mostly they talked Welsh, but occasionally one would speak English to me with a friendly grin.

'I hope you're not bored,' said a cheerful-looking boy with red hair. 'Our discos aren't always like this. Usually it's only us young ones, so it's a bit more sophisticated!'

'I believe you!' I assured him. 'Anyway, I like it.'

Someone called from the stage at the end of the room and everyone began to form a large circle.

'It's a folk dance,' said Glyn. 'Don't worry, just follow what everyone else does.'

I got it right most of the time, which was more than some of them did. When somebody stepped the wrong way and muddled the others up, everyone laughed and took it as a joke, so it was all great fun. At one point we had to swap partners and I found myself face-to-face with a succession of grinning strangers of all ages.

I released the hand of a fat bald man in a checked shirt to find myself being whirled round by a dark-haired young guy who seemed vaguely familiar. As we stopped turning and took two steps to the left, he smiled at me.

'You're a visitor, aren't you. What's your name?'

'Jacky. At the risk of sounding corny, haven't I seen you somewhere before?'

He nodded, looking pleased. But before he could say any more we had to change partners again and soon I was back in Glyn's arms, being whirled round at breathless speed.

When that dance ended there was a break for refreshments. Unfortunately, Gelert, who had sat quietly in a corner while we danced, seemed to think it was time for his refreshment as well and insisted on licking my legs again.

'You seem to have made a conquest there,' Glyn commented. 'Funny, he didn't make much fuss of you yesterday.'

'It takes time to appreciate my charms.' I carried on eating my sausage roll as if nothing was wrong. But looking down at my legs I saw with horror a broad white streak on my left shin where the dog had licked.

'Excuse me,' I said hastily and disappeared into the toilet. At the wash-basin was a friendly looking girl called Gwen to whom Glyn had introduced me earlier on.

'Hi,' she said, turning round from combing her short black hair in the mirror.

'Hi. That dog's been licking my make-up off.' I wet my hands and rubbed my leg, trying to blend the remaining colour more evenly to cover the pale bit.

'Oh, make-up is it? I thought you'd been abroad to get that lovely colour. Never mind, it's OK now. I won't give you away.'

She began to giggle. 'I've only just noticed, when you're bending down like that. You've got a big white

66

patch on the back of your neck too! Who's been licking you there, then?'

'Not Glyn. That stupid mutt again.'

'I should hope it wasn't Glyn, or you'll be in trouble with Moira when she gets back.' I didn't reply.

'Mind you, I think they're cooling off a bit these days,' Gwen added. 'But you're only here for a couple of weeks, so it wouldn't be of any interest to you.'

'That's right. Glyn's just showing me around.' Was it true, I wondered. And who was doing the cooling off – him or her? Gwen was right about one thing. It really didn't matter, because even if Glyn had been madly in love with me we'd never see each other again after next week.

'Here, if you let your hair down at the back like this it will cover that white patch,' suggested Gwen helpfully. So I took out the ribbon and the hair grips and combed it out.

'I wondered what kept you so long,' said Glyn when I returned to the table. 'Now I see you were changing your hairstyle. I like it better that way. I hate girls who try to look sophisticated.'

'Well, I don't choose my hairstyles just to please you.'

An old fifties record boomed out and some of the older folk began rock and rolling. Gradually the younger ones joined in too. Glyn grinned.

'A pony tail's what you need for this!' He slipped his hand up the back of my neck and held my hair up high. 'Mm. That suits you.'

I didn't reply. My neck tingled as though his touch

had electrified it. I hoped I wasn't blushing. He let my hair fall and took my hand.

'Are you feeling energetic? Come on, let's go.'

We danced right through several old fifties, sixties and seventies numbers. There was much more space on the floor now, as many people had left and several others were sitting out. Glyn danced with enthusiasm, pausing now and again to utter some wisecrack about the old fogeys, one of his friends, or the man on the loudspeaker.

He seemed to be enjoying this evening as much as I was. Certainly, the absent Moira appeared to be far from his thoughts, as his blue eyes laughed into mine. Was he just a flirt?

The music changed to a slow, smoochy waltz. Several couples sat down and I looked quizzically at Glyn. Most boys I knew didn't like old-fashioned ballroom dancing. But he made a mock bow and said, 'May I have the pleasure?'

I nodded. 'As long as you don't mind me treading on your toes.'

'Not at all. I know who'll win that game because my shoes are tougher than yours.' Everything was a game to Glyn, I thought. Sometimes his continual banter seemed like fencing, to keep me at bay.

We waltzed round very properly, without taking any wrong steps, ignoring his mates who were grinning at us from the sidelines. Over Glyn's broad shoulder, I glimpsed the face of the dark-haired boy who had partnered me briefly in the barn dance. Where had I seen him before?

The lights were dimmed, another waltz was played,

Glyn's friends drifted back to the floor or away to chat in corners. The other couples still dancing were mostly locked in each other's arms now, shuffling dreamily to the music. My mind began to weave fantasies of being Glyn's girlfriend. As if sensing my thoughts, his arm tightened round my back, drawing me closer.

My fingers quivered on his shoulder, longing to move from his T-shirt to the bare, brown skin of his neck. But I told myself that I mustn't, that he wasn't my boyfriend, he belonged to another girl. His warm breath caressed my ear as he whispered, 'I love your perfume. What is it?'

'Reverie,' I whispered back. Then I remembered that other, more subtle aroma which Gelert's sharp nostrils had detected, and had to suppress a giggle.

Glyn stiffened, stared at me in annoyance and drew back.

'I'm tired of dancing. Let's sit down,' he said abruptly. I followed him to a seat, not holding hands this time. He sat gazing coldly at the dancers, ignoring me. I wanted to explain why I'd giggled, that I wasn't making fun of him, but couldn't bear to let him know what an idiot I'd been.

When the last waltz was announced, he stood up and said he'd take me home. I felt deflated, as if I'd spoilt the evening, and yet relieved. At least I hadn't behaved in a way I'd regret later. The last thing I wanted to do was steal someone else's boyfriend.

We drove off in stony silence. Soon Gelert, in the back seat, began his neck licking routine again. I moved out of his way.

'Sit!' commanded Glyn in a stern voice. After that the dog sat without moving.

'Why on earth didn't you say that to him on the way here?' I demanded. Glyn turned his eyes from the road for a moment to stare at me in surprise.

'I didn't think you minded him licking you. You were smiling and looked as if you were enjoying it.'

I tried very hard to think up a suitable retort but failed utterly. The more I thought about it, in fact, the more I saw the funny side of it. By the time we'd arrived back I'd started giggling again.

Glyn switched the engine off. 'I HATE girls who giggle mysteriously over nothing. If there really is a joke, maybe you'd care to share it with me.'

So I told him all about the gravy-browning, my discomfiture at the dog's unwelcome attentions, the repair job in the loo. He stared in amazement and disbelief.

'Gravy-browning! Well, I wondered why on earth you'd put that brown gunge on, but I assumed it was make-up.'

'So you *were* taking the mickey on the way there, when you said I'd caught the sun.'

'Well, of course. You could hardly have turned into a sun-bronzed goddess overnight.'

I flushed and bit my lip. I'd never felt such an idiot in my life. Glyn looked at my expression, and started to laugh. Soon I couldn't resist joining him. We laughed till the tears rolled down our cheeks.

'I'll say one thing for Gelert,' quipped Glyn, 'he's got good taste! I wonder what it does taste like . . .

woof, woof!' He suddenly began to lick my neck and the bare parts of my shoulders, making doggy noises.

'Don't! Stop it. STOP IT!' I shrieked. His antics were arousing very disturbing feelings in me. He put his hand over my mouth.

'Sh-sh-sh. They'll think I'm raping you!'

The last thing I wanted was mum and dad and Mrs Rees rushing out to see what was the matter, so I stopped pushing him away and screaming. I slumped back against the seat, giggling helplessly.

His tongue was exploring my ear now. He wasn't making silly noises any more. I stopped laughing and my breath came faster. All at once it was serious. His lips moved lightly across my cheek and on to mine. My arms went round his neck, drawing him closer, and we locked in a deep and passionate embrace that seemed to last an eternity.

It was I who pulled away first, breaking the spell.

'I must go now. They'll be wondering what's keeping us.' I couldn't help thinking about the previous night, when I stood at my window, watching this same car in the same spot.

As I stepped out, he held my hand for a moment.

'Jacky, I don't know what to say . . .'

'Don't say anything.' I kissed him lightly on the forehead, released his hand and ran to the bungalow without looking back.

Chapter 11

'Jacky, Jacky, wake up!' someone was shaking me. Confused, I struggled to sit up and rub the sleep from my eyes. It was Cath, waving a bucket and spade at me. The sun was streaming in through the French windows, dazzling me. I looked at the little travel clock on my bedside table. Six-thirty.

I groaned. 'Cath, it's still the middle of the night. Go back to sleep.'

'It isn't! It isn't! It's a lovely hot day and we're all going on the beach.'

'Yes, I expect so, but not just now. First you go back to bed for a little while, then we'll all get up and have breakfast.'

Cath pouted. 'It can't be night. The sun's shining.'

I sighed. 'Look, Cath, it's summer, and in summer sometimes the sun shines very early. OK? Now go back to bed and let me get back to sleep.'

She trotted off. About to turn over and put the pillow over my head to keep out the sunlight streaming through the flimsy curtains, I suddenly recalled the events of last night. I sat bolt upright.

Not only had I allowed Glyn to kiss me, I'd actually responded enthusiastically! Knowing perfectly well that he was only passing the time with me while

Moira was away. As if he wasn't conceited enough already, I'd now given him reason to believe that I was just another moonstruck dolly-bird chasing after him. Whatever had possessed me to behave like that?

I resolved to tell him, the next time we met, that it hadn't meant a thing. And to refuse any more dates with him.

I was trying in vain to get back to sleep when the doorbell rang. Whoever could it be so early in the morning?

Cath came in again, but without the bucket and spade this time. 'It's Glyn. He wants to talk to you.'

'What, now? Does he know what time it is?'

Cath shrugged. I leaped out of bed, my heart pounding, and looked at myself in the mirror. The brown stuff washed away, I looked my usual pale self. I combed my hair and put on my dressing-gown. Had Glyn come to say what I intended saying to him? That he was sorry, but it hadn't meant anything? Or – had he come to say something quite different?

The front door was swinging open, but there was no one in sight. I went out and looked both ways. No one. I glanced across at the house next door, but there was no sign of life. In the room which I assumed was Glyn's bedroom, from which he'd leaned out and waved to me that first day, the curtains were drawn.

I turned round to see Cath standing in the doorway trying to stifle a giggle in her hand. With mounting fury I realized she'd played a joke.

'Cath, you rang the bell yourself, didn't you?'

She nodded, looking serious and apprehensive. I

remembered how bored I used to get when I was her age if I woke up early when everyone else was asleep. She wasn't to know how wrong a morning it was for such a joke!

So I gave up the idea of going back to sleep, told Cathy to get dressed while I slipped into jeans and a sweater, and took her for an early morning walk along the deserted beach. I'd half hoped, in spite of myself, that Glyn might be taking Gelert for a walk too, but there was no sign of them.

It was beautiful weather, just as Cath had forecast, and after breakfast we all went down to the beach again, except for Dad, who'd gone hill-walking on his own. He'd asked me to join him, but I'd declined. I had to see Glyn, just to set the record straight, only I wanted it to be a casual meeting on the beach. Surely, he was bound to come here on such a fine day.

'I'm going for a stroll round to the next cove,' I announced after lunch. Tired of building sandcastles and teaching Paul to swim, I took my towel and clothes, walked to the headland and climbed over the rocks. Passing the cave Glyn had shown me that first morning, I imagined it as a setting for a love scene in my novel, between Megan and Owain.

Then, looking round the ribbed walls and sandy, seaweedy floor, I had the idea of bringing Megan back here later on her own, when she was feeling sad and lonely because Owain was engaged to Amber. Engrossed in her solitary musings, she would forget where she was and get caught by the tide. Owain would arrive in the nick of time to save her by making the hazardous climb down the sheer cliff face, and that would bring the two of them back together again. I suppose it was Glyn's account of the mock rescue that made me think of it.

After that I left the cave quickly, just in case I should get too engrossed in my solitary musings! I rounded the headland to the next sandy cove where a group of teenagers were taking turns on a wind-surfer. I recognized some of them as Glyn's friends whom I'd met at the disco last night. But he wasn't with them. The dark-haired boy I'd danced with was, though. Gwen waved to me with a friendly smile.

'Hi there! Coming in the water, Jacky?'

I nodded. I was already in my swimsuit, so I just dumped the rest of my gear on the sand and joined them. They were talking Welsh, but changed to English when I came up to them. Somehow, that made me feel uncomfortable, as if they'd been discussing me, which I knew was silly, but I couldn't help it.

I swam around for a while, then the dark-haired boy asked me if I'd like a turn on the windsurf board.

'Well, I've never tried it before,' I said doubtfully. The board, bobbing up and down on the waves, looked very unstable, and the pink sail lying flat on the water looked very large and unwieldy.

'There's a first time for everyone,' the boy urged. 'Come on, have a go. I'll tell you what to do.'

'OK, then,' I agreed. After all, what did it matter if I fell off?

'Now this pointed end is the front, and it doesn't matter whether it's on your left or right. Now the foot facing the front is your front foot and the other is your back foot, never mind whether they're left or right. Got that?'

I nodded. That seemed simple enough.

'Right. You always put your front foot on first, then your back foot, balancing with one each side of the centre and half-way across the width of the board like this. Then try and balance crouching down. Just try that.'

I got on the board as he'd told me and rather to my surprise found that I could balance in a crouching posture without falling off.

'That was the easy bit!' he laughed. 'Now you've got to get the sail up without overbalancing. Pick up the rope keeping your arms straight and letting your legs take the strain as you get up from the crouching position. When you've got the sail half-way up, pause to let the water run off. That makes it lighter, then you can pull it the rest of the way up more easily.'

But this time I didn't even get the sail as far as half-way up before I lost my balance and toppled over backwards with a splash! Everyone cheered. I felt a bit of an idiot until my self-appointed tutor, whose name was John, said everyone did that at first. I had another go and this time he showed me how to make sure the wind was blowing from behind me. After a couple of tries I got the sail up – then immediately fell in again! Next time the sail and I stayed vertical by some miracle, and John explained how to turn the sail and use the wind to steer in the direction of the headland.

I pointed my front foot the way I was going and

tried to hold the sail at the right angle. All of a sudden the light breeze seemed to be right with me and I skimmed along the water feeling like a bird in flight.

I could hear the others cheering and shouting, 'Well done!' and, 'Isn't she going well?' It felt great! Then, as I kept going in the direction of the headland, I began to wonder how to stop. John hadn't told me how yet! Visions of myself and the surfboard crashing on to the rocks aroused a sudden panic. I let go and jumped off.

'Why did you do that?' shouted John. 'You were doing so well!'

He and the others swam towards where I was treading water, clinging to the board in case it got swept out to sea, and John climbed on. I admired the neat way he swung it round and sailed swiftly back to the shallows where I'd set off. I followed, with Gwen swimming by my side.

'That was really good,' she said. 'You're getting the hang of it now.'

'John's a patient teacher,' I said. She nodded.

'Yes, I know. He taught me last summer. He's been windsurfing for years. He even does it in winter, in a wet suit. That's his board you were on, by the way.'

Someone else was having a go on it now. 'He's very generous to let everyone borrow it,' I commented.

'Yes, he's like that. He's got his own car and he often lets friends borrow that as well.'

After the others had had turns on the windsurfer, John encouraged me to have another go. Again he helped me with well-timed advice and I succeeded in going about a hundred yards in another direction before trying to turn round and falling off.

John himself then had a go and, beginning to feel chilled, I left the water to stretch myself out on the sand. The sun shone warmly on my back and legs. It felt quite strong so I put on some suntan oil. As I was rubbing it into my shoulders, Gwen joined me.

'Want me to do your back?' she offered.

'Thanks.' How friendly they all were, I thought. I was really lucky to have met them.

'You're good on the surfboard,' I told Gwen. 'I've been watching you from here.'

'Oh, I'm just a beginner. John and Glyn are experts. And so's Moira. I'm just not in their class at all.'

Moira again. I imagined her tall, suntanned figure gracefully balanced on a surfboard. Why did I keep getting this feeling of having to compete with her — and failing?

Chapter 12

As I climbed the steep granite steps from the beach up to our bungalow, I could see that my family had gone. The still-bright sun was weaker now, throwing my elongated shadow before me.

I'd really enjoyed my afternoon, in spite of Glyn

not being there. Thinking of how helpful John had been, I pictured in my mind's eye his slight brown figure, glistening with seawater, his dark, Latin looks. Suddenly I realized where I'd seen him before — he was the boy in the pub where we'd stopped for lunch on the way here.

But why hadn't Glyn been on the beach with his friends today? It wasn't as though he had Moira to go around with. Was he fishing or walking the dog?

Ascending the last few steps, which gave me a view of the Rees' house as well as our bungalow, I received an answer to my question. Glyn's tall, muscular figure, clad only in a pair of brief denim shorts, was hoeing the borders of his garden. A glance at the bungalow garden showed me that he'd been at work there too. The lawns were freshly cut and the flower beds and borders weeded.

'All right for some!' he remarked with a smile, straightening up as he saw me. 'Wish I'd had time for the beach.'

'The beach is here for you whenever you like,' I retorted. 'I have to make the most of my two weeks.'

His expression turned serious. 'Two weeks ... look, I'm sorry about last night. I didn't intend it to happen. Holiday romances are pointless, after all.'

The sensible little speech I'd prepared flew out of my mind. I felt my lips begin to quiver and that prickly feeling in my eyes that comes before tears.

'Yes, well ... I've got to go now.' I turned and ran the rest of the way to the bungalow. In the bathroom I splashed cold water on my face and took several deep breaths to calm myself.

'Did you have a nice time on your own, love?' asked mum as I entered the sunny dining-kitchen.

'Yes, thanks. I spent the afternoon with some friends of Glyn.'

'That's nice for you. Are you seeing them again tomorrow?'

'I don't know.' I hadn't thought about it. Glyn might be with them tomorrow. I'd like to join Gwen, John and the others, and I was looking forward to having another go at windsurfing. But could I cope with Glyn being there too, behaving as if nothing had happened?

'What do you want for tea? We just had beans on toast.'

'It's OK, Mum, I'll get it. And I'll wash up while you put Paul and Cath to bed.'

'You're beginning to turn brown,' dad remarked with a grin. 'Naturally, I mean, not out of a bottle this time.'

I ignored him. Wasn't anyone going to let me forget it? Thank goodness he didn't know *which* bottle it came out of, or the trouble with the dog, or I would never have heard the end of it.

Feeling hungry after my efforts on the surfboard, I fried bacon and eggs to go with my baked beans on toast. Dad watched in amusement.

'You're going to get so fat you'll go down like a stone when you try to swim tomorrow.'

'You're only jealous because you know I can eat anything I like without getting fat.' Secretly, I wished I could put on some weight. I felt self-conscious about being skinny in my swimsuit. I didn't dare wear a skimpy bikini like Gwen, because my ribs showed. I envied her smooth, tanned midriff and rounded bust.

I decided to change the subject. 'Why don't you and mum go in the water?'

'We did. We both had a paddle after you'd gone.'

'Oh, Dad! I mean properly, in swimsuits. You never do.'

'Well, we never learnt to swim, lass. There weren't so many swimming-pools around when we were young.'

'I know, but it's never too late. You'll never learn if you don't try.'

He shook his head, laughing. 'No, you can't teach an old dog new tricks. Up to my knees is far enough for me!'

After I'd finished eating I washed up and dad dried. From the bathroom I could hear Cath wailing over something, and mum trying to calm her down. She really was in a mood!

Dad was gazing out of the kitchen window at the hills, which were beginning to turn rosy against the darkening sky.

'Isn't that a grand view, lass?'

'Yes, it's beautiful.'

'Imagine looking out on that every day. How would you like to live round here?'

I hesitated. Dad was trying to get me on his side in his argument with mum. 'I'd love it. But there's not much work around here and maybe mum's right about your being too young to retire.'

'But if we got a bigger house we could keep visitors all summer, and maybe at Easter too. That would be plenty of work for both of us. There's no difference these days between men's work and women's work. Leastways, that's what you're always telling me.'

I laughed. 'I never realized you took any notice! I thought everything I said went in through one ear and out through the other with you old fogeys.'

'I'll have less of that cheek!' retorted dad, playfully flicking the teatowel at me. 'But seriously, don't you think it's a good idea?'

'Yes, it sounds fine to me. But it's mum you have to persuade.'

'Well, then, you persuade her. If we lived around here you could see that young man next door all the time. You'd even be going to the same school.'

'Dad, I am not, repeat not, in love with Glyn!' I lied. 'Anyway, he's got a steady girlfriend. And as for buying a house here, I am not taking sides with either you or mum and that's the end of it.'

'All right, all right, I surrender.' Dad pretended to back off in alarm. 'But if you don't mind my saying so, I think young Glyn has his eye on you too.'

I gave up and went to my room for some peace and quiet. Dad was so wrong about that. If he'd seen how Glyn smiled and flirted with any female between six and sixty, he wouldn't say such ridiculous things. Anyway, he'd say anything to get me on his side.

It was time to write some more of my historical romance. The love scene in the cave was going quite well when I was distracted by the scent of burning. Going to the window, I saw Glyn setting fire to some garden rubbish. I stepped back hastily. I didn't want him to think I was watching him. But I did watch from behind the curtain as he raked more grass into the leaping flames, pausing to wipe the sweat from his face with the back of his arm. He really was the most attractive boy I'd ever met. There was no denying it. I sighed, and was about to turn back to Owain and Megan when the little castle on the horizon caught my eye once more.

This time it was later in the evening, and its silhouette was black against the violet sky. In the foreground flames from Glyn's bonfire leapt upwards, bringing to mind my *Castles in the Fire* image more vividly than ever. The crumbling, tumbling towers and turrets. My vain daydreams about Glyn, my foolish hopes of being a writer, all going up in flames, turning to ashes . . .

Dad's words to me in the kitchen flashed into my mind.

'You'd even be going to the same school.'

He seemed to be taking it for granted that I was going into the sixth form. But I hadn't yet made up my mind. If I did A levels I'd have lots of homework, which meant I'd have very little time to do any writing. I wished I could discuss my real ambition with my parents, as I had with Glyn's mum.

I wondered if dad would get his way about coming here to live. Would Glyn's attitude to me be different if it wasn't just a 'holiday romance'? He hadn't mentioned Moira. But he was obviously worried about possible trouble when she returned. Maybe he'd thought we were staying just this week, that I'd be gone before Moira came back on the scene.

With a sigh, I turned my attention to my hero

and heroine once more. Soon I'd left the present completely and was totally immersed in the nineteenth century. Planning the cave-rescue scene in my mind, I jotted some notes about it on a separate sheet of paper, as I hadn't come to that bit yet. I wanted to save it for my climax.

In the meantime, I'd reached the part where Megan hears that Glyn (whoops! I crossed it out and wrote in 'Owain') is to marry the beautiful and wealthy Amber. As I scribbled on, I felt Megan's plight more and more keenly, until eventually I found myself in tears! Looking into the dressing-table mirror, I watched the glistening blobs roll slowly down my cheeks. Then I started laughing at myself, wondering what dad would say if he could see me now! It was the first time I'd actually cried when writing a story, and in a funny way I enjoyed it, like you do when watching a sad film.

Who was I kidding? I knew the real reason for those tears. Drawing a line under the chapter end, I went to the window again.

Far in the west, over the sea, the violet clouds were still faintly tinged with crimson. Next door, a few embers glowed in the black, deserted garden. Red sky at night . . . what would tomorrow bring?

Chapter 13

A scorcher. For once the old 'shepherd's delight' chestnut turned out to be true. The sun glared through the picture windows from a cloudless sky on to the breakfast table. The milk turned and the butter ran.

We all made for the beach again, including dad this time. I left them to make my way round the headland to the cove where I'd met Glyn's friends yesterday. It was deserted — apart from Glyn and Gelert. The latter was running and barking in the shallows, while Glyn, looking like a bronzed god in blue swim trunks, threw pebbles for him to chase.

I paused on the rocks, meaning to turn back before he saw me. But he looked up and smiled. 'Come on in, Jacky! Gelert tells me the water's lovely.'

Still hesitating, I hoped he didn't think I'd come here on purpose to seek him out. But now he'd seen me it would be childish to run away, back to my parents. I slipped out of my shorts and T-shirt and ran down to the water's edge. The dog rushed up, wagging his tail, shaking himself and showering me with droplets.

'Ouch! I'm not sure I believe you about the water, Gelert. It feels pretty cold to me.' I felt self-conscious in my regulation-style black swimsuit, remembering the colourful bikinis Gwen and the other girls had sported yesterday. But I was determined to be very cool with Glyn, to behave as though nothing had happened between us.

I plunged into the sea and struck out swiftly. It was surprisingly cold after the heat of the beach. A sound of splashing behind me made me turn round. Glyn was fast catching up with me, his muscular brown arms cleaving the water with powerful strokes.

'Where are you going, Jacky – Ireland?'

'We're not that far out.'

'No, but we soon will be if you keep this pace up!'

I was about to think up a suitable retort, when I heard voices on the beach. Gwen, John, a red-haired boy called Eric, and another couple whose names I didn't remember were throwing a ball around. I waved to them and they waved back.

'It's your friends. Let's go and join them.'

'What's the hurry, Jacky? Stay here and talk to me.'

'I don't think I've anything to say. You said it all yesterday.' With that, I turned and swam back to the shore, but Glyn overtook me and arrived there first. He didn't look too pleased. I thought maybe I wasn't the only one who swam better when I was angry.

'Hi there!' Gwen greeted us. 'We're all off to Nant Garregog today. It's the only place that won't be overcrowded. Are you two coming?'

Glyn stood up, shaking the water from his hair. 'No, we'll stay here and do some windsurfing. I'm sure Jacky would like to have a go. It's impossible to take our boards to the Nant except by sea.'

'I'd love to join you lot,' I put in quickly. 'I've wanted to see that place ever since Glyn told me about it on my first day here.' I was amazed that Glyn could take so much for granted after what he'd said yesterday — and determined not to spend the day alone with him.

'Fine,' said Gwen. 'Come as you are. All you need is a packed lunch.'

'I've got one, thanks.'

'How about you, Glyn? Won't you change your mind and come with us? Jacky had a go at wind-surfing yesterday, by the way. John gave her some lessons and she got on really well.'

The smile dropped from Glyn's face. 'Thanks, but I'll stay here all the same. Come on, boy!'

Whistling to Gelert, he ran off along the beach with the dog bounding after him. I stared after him, wondering if windsurfing was the real reason for his not wanting to join the others.

'Never mind him,' said Gwen. 'I expect he's annoyed that you're not crazy about him like all the other visitors.'

'The others?' I tried not to sound as anxious as I felt.

John laughed. 'There was a girl who stayed in that bungalow last summer — Debbie, her name was, I think — and she followed him around everywhere just like the dog!'

The others laughed and I pretended to join in, though I was beginning to blush, remembering that kiss in the car. He must have thought I was an easy conquest, just like the others.

My heart was heavy as we set off along the cliff road, but soon the sunshine and the bright chatter of the others raised my spirits. When we came to the tangle of bushes and pine trees that hid the way down to the secret bay, I no longer had time to think about Glyn. The steepness of the track down the cliff face needed all our concentration.

About half-way down, the trees and bushes opened out and we could see the deserted village with its cluster of derelict cottages, all built of rough slabs of local granite, many with their mossy slate roofs caved in. The footpath widened into a rough road leading between the houses down to a beautiful bay completely surrounded by massive cliffs, uncompromisingly sheer except for the winding path we'd descended.

John followed my upward gaze. 'It's totally invisible from above. Those dense thickets on the cliff have always hidden it.'

I stared round at the silent ruins, the magnificent, mile-long crescent of sand, the calm sea unbroken by sail or swimmer.

'I can't believe it – we've got the whole place to ourselves!'

'Yippee!' cried Eric, doing a cartwheel on the beach. The other couple, whose names I'd now learned were Olwen and Dai, stripped down to their swimsuits and ran into the sea.

I was already in mine, not having bothered to get dressed for the walk and the climb down, but I felt too exhausted for a swim just yet. I spread my towel and lay on my back, gazing up into the clear, blue sky.

John sat next to me. 'Have you remembered yet where you've seen me before?'

'Yes. You were having lunch in a pub we stopped at on the way here. Were those your parents with you?'

He nodded. 'We were on our way back from holiday.'

'Seems strange to think of someone living in a place like this going away on holiday!'

'Well, we don't go to the seaside. This year we went to London for shops and theatres and things.'

I laughed. 'That's ridiculous — going to London for your summer holiday.'

'Not for us. It's a change.'

But the real reason for my laughter was remembering that absurd daydream I'd had of falling in love with this guy. Not that he wasn't nice looking, or pleasant company, but there was none of that tension, that excitement I felt when I was with Glyn. John was just a pal, like Gwen and the others. That was all.

We all had a great time that day, swimming, sunbathing and just fooling around. The only hard bit was climbing back up the cliff path — it took us twice as long as it had to come down. I was grateful for John's help to pull me up one particularly steep part.

As we straggled back along the cliff road, John made a point of walking next to me, although he didn't say much. I began to realize he was quite a shy person who found it easier to give practical instructions, like when he was teaching me to wind-surf, than to make light conversation.

When we reached the place where the track forked off for the bungalow, the others said goodbye and went on ahead, but John lingered.

'Perhaps we could go somewhere together while you're here,' he ventured. 'There must be some other local sights you'd like to visit. I'd be glad to show you around.'

He'd obviously spent some time plucking up courage for this little speech, so I didn't want to hurt his feelings by saying a definite no.

'Thanks, that's nice of you. I'd love to visit Caer-narvon Castle some time. Perhaps we could all go together, if the others agree.'

His face fell, but he said, 'Yes, great. I'll ask them.'

'I can see the castle from my bedroom window. Look, you can just see it from here as well.'

His gaze followed my pointing finger. 'That's not Caernarvon Castle, that's a folly!'

Chapter 14

'Worth the climb, wasn't it?'

I nodded, gazing down at the countryside spread out below us like a map, the coastline shaded around with too bright a blue. Another perfect day and only the two of us here to enjoy it together. Our eyes met and we smiled happily.

This mountain peak could be seen from the kitchen window of our bungalow, and I'd longed to stand on the summit. We'd had to take the car along winding country roads to the farmhouse at the foot of it where the steep upward path began. Dad knew it would be too tiring for mum, Paul and Cath so they'd opted to spend another day on the beach.

I'd felt the need to get away from Gwen, John and the rest. Even from Glyn. Especially from Glyn. I remembered the cold look he'd given me when Gwen referred to John teaching me to windsurf. Why? One possible explanation made my heart beat faster, and not just because of the climb I'd completed. Maybe he was jealous.

'You're dreaming again,' said dad, sitting down and removing his rucksack. 'What is it this time? Thinking of your lunch, or that young fellow next door?'

'You were right the first time,' I lied. 'Come on, let's eat. I'm starving.'

'You are keen on him, though, aren't you?' dad insisted, getting out the lunch he'd packed earlier on, and a bottle of Coke. Salami sandwiches, cheese and crackers, a pork pie cut in two and a couple of ripe, juicy peaches.

'That looks good!' I remarked, not answering his question. I tucked into a piece of pie as if I hadn't heard. He took the other half.

'The reason I'm asking is that I get the impression

he feels the same way about you,' he went on. 'And Mrs Rees was saying on the beach yesterday that although he gives the appearance of being a bit big-headed, it's only because he's really shy. She thought he might be attracted to you as well.'

My heart leaped. But I tried my best to sound very cool.

'Might be! And then again he might not. The fact is, Dad, he's already got a girlfriend.'

'She can't be very keen on him if she goes off to stay with school friends as soon as she gets home. With her being at boarding school most of the year the holidays are the only times they have to be together. I think he told her as much the night before she went. They came in looking sulky and her eyes were red as if she'd been crying.'

I thought back to the evening when we'd had dinner with Ann Rees and I'd gone back to the bungalow with the kids. I'd assumed Glyn was kissing Moira when they stayed in the car for half an hour before going in the house. But maybe they'd been quarrelling?

'That was the second night we were here,' I said thoughtfully. 'Why didn't you mention this before?'

He shrugged. 'Your Mum told me to keep out of it, mind my own business and not go stirring up trouble. She was afraid of someting like that business with Robert happening all over again.'

'Aren't you? It must have been just as upsetting for you.'

'Well, I reckon you're older and wiser now. You're

getting to be a real sensible lass most of the time. Apart from the daydreaming.'

'Gee, thanks! Coming from you, that must be a compliment.'

'Besides, Glyn isn't a silly baby of a lad like Robert. He'll be eighteen on Friday. He's a great help to his mother with that house, does all the repairs and decorating for her, in the bungalow as well, and keeps both the gardens looking nice.'

'He'll make someone a good husband, then, won't he?'

'Oh, aye. A feller that's good to his mother will be good to his wife. That's what I always say. What are you laughing at?'

'Well, he's hardly eighteen yet, and you've already got him married off! I think you've taken a fancy to him as a son-in-law and now you're trying to engineer a romance between us.'

After we'd finished lunch and dad had taken some photos of the view we began the long trek down the mountain. It was only slightly easier than climbing up and the sun was very warm. I hoped my arms and legs would get tanned, as I was wearing only brief shorts and a T-shirt.

By the time we reached the farmhouse at the foot of the hill it was nearly five. There was a 'Teas' sign outside, so we stopped for a cool drink and an ice-cream before getting into the car.

Dad returned to what was his favourite subject these days: his plans to give up his job back home and settle somewhere round here.

'I reckon now's the time. Once you start your A

levels you'll have to stay in the same school for two years.'

'But Dad, I haven't decided about that yet. You see, I want to be a writer.' I don't know why my secret came out, just like that, but it did. Maybe it was something to do with the fine weather, the comfortable atmosphere in the little cafe, or dad's good mood. To my surprise, he didn't laugh.

'Well, why not? Your teachers say that you write well. And I suppose you're scribbling away when you spend so much time in your bedroom.'

'I didn't know you guessed! The point is, if I'm always studying I won't have time to write.'

'I should think you'll manage, a clever girl like you. And you'll need A levels if you're going to be a journalist on a newspaper or magazine.'

That hadn't occurred to me. 'But I want to be a novelist. Or a short-story writer.'

'That sounds like a lonely occupation for a young girl. Why not be a journalist and write fiction in your spare time?'

'I hadn't thought about it. Maybe I should go to the careers office and find out when we get back.'

'Good idea.'

That evening, after dinner, I took what I'd written so far of my novel round to Mrs Rees. As she welcomed me into her cosy kitchen, I noticed Gelert asleep in a big dog basket in the corner.

'Glyn left him behind tonight because he was fast asleep after his day on the beach,' explained Ann.

'Oh, is Glyn out? That's good, because I wanted to discuss my novel with you, if you're not too busy.'

'No, not at all. Sit down and have a cup of tea. So that's your *Castles in the Fire*. Sounds interesting.'

While she was pouring out the tea I asked, 'Talking of castles, someone told me the one I can see from my window is a folly. What does that mean?'

'It was built by a wealthy landowner in the eighteenth century, just as a decoration.'

'I always thought it didn't look real, somehow.' I explained to her what my title meant to me, describing the imaginary castles I used to see in the fire when I was younger.

'Castles in the Fire,' she mused, almost as if talking to herself. 'You see them as impossible dreams that can never come true. Crumbling towers and palaces destroyed by fire. Hmm – that's very sad, very negative. But what if that fire is really a crucible? And the castles are not being destroyed but formed there?'

'Pardon?' She'd lost me now. I had no idea what she was talking about. She smiled.

'I was just rambling on, thinking aloud. I do that at times. Take no notice.'

As I was going to bed that night I looked out at the little castle and wondered again at her words. I also wondered about Glyn. Where was he and who had he gone out with? I'd longed to ask Mrs Rees, but didn't want her to think me nosy.

He wasn't mine and I had no right to wonder.

Chapter 15

Lightning split the sky and seconds later thunder threatened to crack open the earth. The curtains billowed into the room, while rain sloshed down the window panes as though a giant were flinging buckets of water from the sky.

From below I could hear the boom of waves crashing against the cliff. I'd gone to sleep with the French windows open and only a sheet over me, because of the heat. Now a chill wind blew right through the room.

I got up and went to shut the window. As I did so another streak of lightning flashed, closely followed by another deafening rumble. Yet I found it hard to tear myself from that window. I was tempted to open it again and run out into the storm. There was something tremendously exciting about the way the moon peered through chinks in the cloud, lighting the spray that leapt almost to the top of the cliff and silvering the crests of mountainous waves that pounded on the beach.

Those waves, especially, fascinated me. The way they rose, swelled greenish-black and opaque in the faint light, erupted into foam and dissolved with a crash into the rest of the sea. This scene simply had to go into *Castles in the Fire*. Although my watch said four-thirty, I sat down at the dressing-table and began to describe the storm. It was the scene where Megan is trapped in the cave at high tide and Owain rescues her. Carried away, I wrote faster and faster . . .

A high wailing sound, louder even than the howl of the wind, could be heard above the crashing of the waves. I paused, wondering what it could be. Some sort of siren?

It stopped, and I could hear other noises through the storm: voices shouting urgently in Welsh, a car pulling up, feet clattering down the steps to the beach. Several lights went on next door.

Rushing to the window, I saw several dark figures scurrying around on the beach below. A couple of others, muffled in macs and sou'westers, ran down our private steps. All over the village lights went on, one after another. More voices, shouting above the wind and rain.

They must be sending the lifeboat out! My heart pounding, I found my mac and wellingtons, tied a scarf round my head and slipped out through the French windows.

I reached the shore seconds after the boat was launched. Among a crowd of other wet, huddled figures, I watched it bob away till the darkness appeared to swallow it up.

'Jacky? I thought it was you.' Glyn's voice made me jump. I spun round to see him grinning from under a black sou'wester dripping rain. In his oilskins and boots he looked as if he should have been on the lifeboat, not just watching it. I said so.

'Yes, we were all hoping there'd be a spare place. There are always more volunteers than they need, that's why we've got the gear on ready, in case one of the regulars was ill or didn't wake up.'

I looked round, my eyes getting accustomed to the dim light, and saw Eric, John and three older men, also in oilskins, gazing out to sea. They must be feeling a sense of anticlimax now, after rushing down here just in case they were needed.

Most of the others on the beach were women, many of them wives, mothers and girlfriends of the lifeboatmen. Some had hastily donned macs over their nighties that trailed in the wet sand, and most wore headscarves. It didn't take much imagination to picture a similar scene a hundred, two hundred years or more ago.

I remembered the disused cemetery on another beach that Glyn had shown me that first day. How there were fewer men's names on the gravestones . . .

'Jacky? Are you still with us? Or are you out at sea with the lifeboat?' Glyn tapped my shoulder. 'I asked if you'd like to come back home with me now. Unless you're waiting for John, that is.'

I stared at him. Strands of wet hair were plastered to his forehead and he was no longer smiling. He WAS jealous, quite absurdly so.

'I'm waiting for the return of the lifeboat, like everyone else. Aren't you?'

'I told mum I'd be back in half an hour if I didn't go out with the boat. If I don't turn up she'll come down to the beach. Will you walk up with me? We can come back afterwards if you like.'

'OK.' I pushed some dangling strands of wet hair back under my scarf, thinking what a mess I must look.

As we walked up the steps he said without looking at me, 'I hear you came round to see mum last night. You must have been surprised that I was out with Gwen.'

I stood still in shock. 'Your mother didn't say where you were, and I didn't ask. But it's none of my business. It's Moira who's going to want explanations.'

He turned to look at me, the mischief dancing in his eyes again, a half-smile lighting up his face.

'But I do flatter myself that you were disappointed, Jacky. You know the way I feel about you and, correct me if I'm wrong, but I got the impression it was mutual. Gwen and I are just old friends, there's nothing between us. I'd have preferred to take you out last night, but since that day on the beach, when you chose not to spend it with me, you seem to have been avoiding me.'

'I thought it was you who was avoiding me! Anyway, I thought we'd agreed not to see each other again because of Moira.'

'Don't stand here, Jacky, you're getting soaked. Come on, we can finish this conversation somewhere more comfortable.'

He took my hand and we ran the rest of the way to his house. He yelled upstairs that he was back and was acknowledged by a drowsy mumble. It was still only six-thirty. Glyn went to the kitchen and put on the kettle.

My scarf was soaked so I took it off and ran my fingers through my wet hair. I didn't want to miss the lifeboat's return, but I also wanted to stay here with Glyn. What had he been trying to tell me? I felt confused.

He poured me a cup of tea, and we sat by the window with the seaward view. 'Perhaps I should have told you, Jacky, that Moira and I quarrelled just before she went away, and we didn't really make it up. We haven't phoned each other at all this week.'

My heart leapt in hope. 'Why didn't you mention this before?' So dad's guess had been right, after all.

'I thought I ought to wait until she returns, to make things clear to her. I feel we've grown away from each other. Inevitable, I suppose, when we're separated for most of the year.'

'As we would be, of course. I'm only here on holiday.'

He grinned ruefully. 'There are so many reasons not to start anything, aren't there? I see you've thought of them as well.'

He took hold of my hand. His clasp tightened and he took my other hand as well, his blue eyes gazing steadily into mine. For a long moment we just sat there, hands and eyes glued to each other's.

'Jacky, I'm not one for holiday romances, but if only things were different, if you lived here, I'd want you to be my girl.'

'I wish I could be.' I felt tears start to prick at the back of my eyes, knowing that I was so near and yet so far from being Glyn's girlfriend. I pulled my hands away, blinking rapidly to dry my eyes.

As I did so, I glanced towards the window, and a new movement on the heaving grey sea caught my attention.

'The lifeboat! It's coming back!'

Glyn put his sou'wester on my head. 'Come on, let's go!'

The pelting rain had slowed to a drizzle now, and the wind had abated. We watched with the others as the four rescued men from the capsized motor-launch were brought ashore. Friends and relatives of the lifeboatmen crowded round and Glyn joined them, leaving me a solitary spectator.

Feeling out of place now, an outsider, and satisfied to know that everyone was safe, I slipped away and went back to the bungalow. I was beginning to feel famished. Also, I was looking forward to telling my family, who had apparently slept through it all, about the exciting drama.

After what Glyn had said, I hoped he'd phone or come round asking me to spend the day with him, but there was no sign of him. So I agreed to go on a trip with my family. We went to see the grave of Gelert, the famous dog after whom Glyn's was named, so that made it all the harder to keep my thoughts from Glyn. I wished we could spend some time together, even if it was to be only a holiday friendship.

That evening, Glyn and his mother had been invited to dinner with us. I'd helped mum prepare it, but most of the skilled cooking was hers and I was really proud of the delicious meal she produced.

Soon the conversation turned to mum and dad's on-going argument, and dad began to put forward his point of view. He mentioned a pleasant five-bedroomed house on the sea front he'd seen for sale.

'A five-bedroomed house!' scoffed mum. 'Our family needs three bedrooms. Do you seriously think two bedrooms could make enough profit to keep us all?'

Dad looked vague. 'Well, maybe a bigger one, then.'

'We'd need a twenty-bedroom mansion to do the job properly. Could we afford it?'

'Er, I haven't thought of actual figures yet,' replied dad, scratching his head. He's losing this one, I thought.

'We shan't need one that big, shall we?'

'I'm afraid you would,' Ann Rees chipped in. 'I've tried bed-and-breakfast, and all you can make is pin-money unless you do it on a large scale.'

'You're out-voted, Mr Nelson,' laughed Glyn. To change the conversation, I began to tell Mrs Rees about my visit to Nant Garregog, the secret village.

'It won't be empty much longer,' she commented. 'The plans for building a proper road down to it have just been passed, I heard today.'

'Oh no!' cried Glyn. 'It'll ruin the place. Trippers everywhere, the beach crowded in summer like any other. Cafés and ice-cream vans, litter on the sand. Why can't they leave it alone?'

'Progress,' she replied with a shrug. Then her

expression changed. 'I've just had a wonderful idea. Why don't you buy a couple of those little ruined cottages and turn them into a café with living quarters?'

'A café!' mum echoed. I could see she was struck with the idea. 'Why, yes. I could do the cooking. I'd love that. There'd be plenty for dad to do as well. And Jacky could help out in the summer holidays, now that she's decided to do A levels.'

Dad grinned. 'Just the job. It's a great idea!'

I looked at Glyn, catching a meaningful glance from his blue eyes. We both smiled. Surely this would change everything!

After dinner Glyn and I put Paul and Cathy to bed, then washed the dishes while his mum and my parents went down to the pub to celebrate their new brainwave. It was obviously a scheme that appealed equally to mum and dad. He had always wanted to live in the country or by the sea, while mum wanted a proper business they could both put their energies into and make a go of.

'Well now, this new development makes all the difference to us, doesn't it?' said Glyn.

'If you're sure about it being over between you and Moira,' I said cautiously, but my voice was trembling with excitement.

He put his hands on my shoulders and looked deep into my eyes. 'Sure I'm sure. We're going to have time together after all. Time to really get to know each other.' He moved his hand to my chin and tilted my face upward.

'Glyn! Jacky! Did the little ones settle down all

right?' It was my dad's voice. I sighed. Surely they couldn't be back already.

'Yes, Mr Nelson, they went out like a light. And everything's ship-shape in the kitchen.'

'That's very nice of you,' said mum, smiling warmly at him.

'Actually, I'm nearly flaking out myself,' I said. 'I've been up since four this morning!'

'Me too,' said Glyn. 'Thank you for a lovely meal, Mrs Nelson.'

'Yes, if that's anything to go by, your home-cooking at the café will be very popular,' added his mother. 'I'm afraid Glyn's party buffet will be an anticlimax after that, but I'll do my best.'

'Oh, I'll cook one or two things for you here and bring them over to your place,' offered mum.

'No, I couldn't possibly let you do that. You're supposed to be on holiday.' Then Mrs Rees noticed that I was staring blankly.

'Glyn, have you told Jacky about the party?'

'No, haven't you?'

'What party? Are you having an eighteenth birthday party, Glyn?' I'd wondered about that. When I wasn't wondering about all the other more important things, that is. Glyn slapped a hand against his forehead.

'Oh no! I'm so sorry, Jacky. I was quite sure my mother or your parents would have told you.'

'Well, naturally we thought you'd told her. But her mum was just saying it's odd she hasn't told us what she's wearing.'

'Jacky, my sweet, you're invited of course. In fact

you'll be the guest-of-honour. It's tomorrow night. But I'll probably see you before then, so I'll say goodnight.'

As he was going out of the door he added,

'Oh, and it's fancy dress . . .'

Chapter 16

That night I found it hard to sleep, I was so excited. There were so many new things to think about: the café project that mum and dad kept going on about, coming to live here, going to the same school as Glyn. But most important of all was the fact that Glyn loved me. Of course, he hadn't exactly said so, but his meaning had been clear. And he had called me his 'sweet'. I kept thinking of that. I was convinced that if dad hadn't interrupted us at just the wrong moment, Glyn would have kissed me.

But what about this party then? Why on earth hadn't anyone got around to telling me before? What was I going to wear? When I woke next morning I was still wondering about it. Fancy dress, he said. It's not that I was short of ideas. On the contrary, all sorts of daft ideas kept leaping into my mind.

A bookworm? Borrow a load of tyres from a garage and dress myself in them from head to foot (to look like a worm's rings) and just have two hands sticking out, holding a book, and maybe antennae on my forehead. I didn't think worms actually had antennae – though Biology wasn't my hottest subject – but the cartoon one on the Bookworm Club logo had them and that's what I wanted to look like.

Then I thought of the other guests' reactions. People have a way of jumping to the most obvious and boring conclusion.

'Oh, so you've come as the Michelin Man,' they'd say. And I'd probably look like him too. No, that wouldn't do at all. Gwen would probably come in something that made her look very pretty but boring, like a Dresden shepherdess or a Christmas tree fairy.

So I tried to think of something that would look sexy, while showing off my long dark hair which I suppose is my best feature, but something a bit different. A gipsy or Hawaiian girl would be easy and attractive, but predictable. I didn't want to have the same idea as half a dozen others.

'Mum,' I said as we washed the breakfast dishes. 'Do you think I could be a go-go dancer? What would I need?'

She nearly dropped a plate as she stared at me in astonishment. 'But Jacky, I thought you'd decided to be a writer or a journalist. You don't need A levels to be a go-go dancer!'

'I mean for the fancy dress party tonight.'

'Oh, that!' she replied, looking relieved. 'Well, why don't you go as a Christmas tree fairy?'

I gave up. I rejected one idea after another. I had money to buy some material or props, as I'd spent very little of my holiday cash, but it had to be something I could make quickly.

Walking along the cliff top to blow away the cobwebs, I didn't meet Glyn as I'd hoped, but I did get an idea for the party. Looking at the sea reminded me of the storm on the night of the rescue. And that reminded me of Hans Andersen's mermaid story. That was it – I'd be a mermaid! Pretty but different. I remembered the other one-piece swimsuit I'd brought with me but hadn't worn. It was made of very thin, clingy material in a peachy shade, and once when I'd worn it at our local swimming baths some boys had teased me, pretending to think I had nothing on, because it was almost flesh-colour.

I could wear that and make a fish's tail to go over it. But how could I walk or dance in a fish's tail? I pondered this problem all the way to the village shops. As I stared in the flyblown window of a little haberdasher's which seemed to sell mainly knitting wool, children's vests, buttons and zip fasteners, the solution came to me. A zip fastener!

I bought a length of shimmering pale-green satin, a long zip fastener, needle and thread, and a couple of yards of buckram for stiffening. At the chemist's next door, which also sold souvenirs and cheap jewellery, I bought a bottle of silver nail varnish, a belt all made of shells, a shell necklace, an imitation coral necklace and bracelet, and two strings of pearls.

For the rest of the day I shut myself away in my room, feverishly cutting, sewing, fixing and trying on. Luckily the weather was fine enough for mum and dad to take Paul and Cath to the beach out of the way.

By late afternoon I hadn't quite finished, but I needed to see Glyn's mum about his present, without him over-hearing. I needn't have worried – he wasn't there.

'He's taken the car to the railway station to pick up Moira,' explained Mrs Rees. 'She's coming back today. It's a thirty-mile journey and the train's often late, so he won't be back for a while. What's this surprise, then?'

I told her about the silver key ring I'd bought Glyn as a present and how I'd left it at Jones the Chemist to have his name engraved on it. In Glanheli the chemist cut keys and engraved jewellery as well as mixing the medicines! Now I was going to fetch it and wanted to take Mrs Rees' front door key and car keys to have copies cut and put on the ring.

'That's very thoughtful of you,' she said. 'I'm sure Glyn will appreciate it.'

But as I walked down to the village again, I began to wonder why I was going to all this trouble. Had I exaggerated Glyn's feelings about me? If he'd gone to pick up Moira it sounded as though he hadn't finished with her after all. And he hadn't actually said so, had he? Surely Moira's parents could have picked her up if necessary.

When the rest of the family were having tea I stayed in my room to finish off my costume. At last it was ready. I'd used the silver varnish to paint scales all over the green satin and it looked very effective. The silvery green tail tapered from my waist to my feet, where I'd made two flaps like the end of a fish tail to slip my sandalled feet into.

The necklaces and garland of real seaweed round my neck and shoulders hid the top of my flesh-coloured swimsuit and from afar it looked as though I was wearing nothing but my tail! One of the pearl necklaces held my hair from my face, like a coronet for a mermaid princess. I wore pearl earrings, pearly green eyeshadow and coral lipstick. And the shell belt, fastened round my waist, hid the top edge of the tail.

With my feet in the flaps and the zip at the side fastened up, the tail looked quite real, but I could only hobble a few steps. If I took my feet out and opened the zip up to my knees, I could walk about normally. So when it was time to go, I ran across the way, holding my fish's tail up like a long skirt to prevent it dragging on the ground, then on the door-step I put my feet in and zipped it up.

One of Glyn's friends opened the door and exclaimed in surprise, 'Well, what do you know, it's a mermaid!'

The others, including Glyn, came crowding round. He was dressed as a fisherman. He laughed when he saw me. Before I knew what was happening, he scooped me up in his arms.

'Hey, put me down!' I cried — although I didn't really want him to.

'I've caught a mermaid!' he murmured in my ear. Then he carried me into a room where a lot of guests were dancing and deposited me on a chair.

'Pity mermaids can't dance!' he remarked. 'I'll go and get you something to eat and drink.'

Several people came over to look curiously at my costume. Most of the others were very conventional, like Glyn. I mean — all he'd had to do was wear jeans and a fisherman's jersey! There were several Welsh ladies with tall hats, a witch, a gypsy, a cavalier, a caveman and three cowboys, at least. When the witch took off her hat I recognized her as Moira. I wondered where Gwen was. A deepsea diver strode up to me and took off his headgear to reveal John.

'A diver and a mermaid should make a good pair,' he said. 'Only mermaids can't dance.'

'This one can!' I retorted, standing up and unzipping my tail. Then we danced round the room, laughing. The others laughed as well, and some of them clapped.

'I vote that one the cleverest costume!' said one of the girls. At that moment Glyn returned with a plate of food and a glass of Coke. He set them down on the chair where I'd been sitting, then went out again. Moira, who'd been sitting down, got up and left the room too.

When the music came to an end I picked up the plate and drink and wandered out. The party seemed to be very lively and going on in several rooms at once. I went into the kitchen where Ann Rees and my mum were doling out food to a queue of hungry-looking folk. Gwen was there too, dressed as a St Trinian schoolgirl with a very short tunic showing lots of black stocking and suspenders. She was busy cutting up a cake.

There was no sign of Glyn. I queued up for a piece of birthday cake, then went back into the room where they were dancing. Glyn wasn't there and neither was Moira. John asked me to dance again, so I did. I didn't want to give the impression that I was just wandering around searching for Glyn.

But of course I was. Eventually I went round every room including the bedrooms, which were empty, one of them piled high with coats. Glyn wasn't anywhere in the house. And neither was Moira.

No longer pretending to enjoy myself, I went out into the garden. At first the fairy lights in the trees dazzled my eyes with their pink, blue and green glow. Then I saw Glyn and Moira.

In a dark corner between a tree and a shed, they were locked in a passionate embrace.

Chapter 17

I meant to run back inside without them seeing me, and lock myself in the loo to cry in private. But in the dark I tripped on a paving stone and Glyn must have heard me.

'What was that?'

'Oh, just someone playing a game. Take no notice.'

'No, I'm going to see who it was . . .' I didn't catch the rest.

Hearing his steps follow me, I ran inside as fast as I could. I was half-way up the stairs when he caught up with me and grabbed my arm.

'Jacky, you've got the wrong idea. It wasn't what you thought.'

'How could I get the wrong idea? I saw you plainly. You and Moira were kissing. You've made up your quarrel. There's nothing else to say. So please let go of my arm.'

I desperately wanted to be released, before I burst into tears. Some of Glyn's friends in the hall were eyeing us curiously. I felt so embarrassed to have my unhappiness made public like this. He let go of my arm.

'Look, Jacky, I must talk to you privately. Please don't run away. You must give me a chance to explain.'

'Where can we go?'

'Come back into the garden with me. Moira isn't there any more. She's gone home.'

'Gone home? So soon? Why?'

'Come outside and I'll explain.'

So I followed him out into the garden, to a seat under a tree. Glyn held my hand and spoke urgently.

'What I told you was true, Jacky. You've got to believe me. I fetched Moira from the train today so that we could have a long talk about the way things have been going for us lately. And we decided not to see each other again. But of course I wanted her to come to my party. What you saw was a goodbye kiss.'

'But if you've split up, I should have thought she'd be too upset to come. I know I would be.'

'But Moira isn't like you. She's very friendly with several boys. You see, she's been writing regularly to the brother of one of her school friends, as well as to me.'

I began to understand. 'Is that the friend she went to stay with?'

'Yes, that's right. Obviously they've been out together during the week she was there, but she wanted to go on seeing me as well. I've told her I just don't want that sort of relationship. So, it's finished. She wanted me to kiss her goodbye for old time's sake, so I did. And that's all there is to it.'

'So that's why she's gone home early.' His words rang true and yes, I believed him. I felt joy bubble up inside me so fast it was hard to remember that a few moments ago I'd been very close to tears.

'Oh, Glyn – I'm so glad you and Moira didn't get back together. Especially now I'm coming to live here.'

His clasp on my hand tightened, he drew me towards him. I felt his warm breath on my cheek as he whispered in my ear, 'It's you I love, Jacky.' Those thrilling words I'd longed to hear!

But as his lips sought mine, a picture flashed into my mind of him and Moira kissing. A goodbye kiss it may have been – and now I firmly believed it was – but it had been long and passionate.

'No, Glyn – not tonight. I don't want you to kiss me yet.' He drew back, looking surprised and hurt. I tried to explain how I felt.

'I mean, not so soon after you kissed Moira. I understand now why you did it. The two of you have been close for a long time and I suppose you can't just switch off all your – your affection for her just like that, but . . .' I trailed off. I couldn't bring myself to say 'love'. He smiled, a tender smile that was different from his usual grin.

'I understand. You're quite right, of course. It was insensitive of me. We'll go out together again very soon. Just the two of us, without all these other people around. Would you like that?'

'Yes, I'd like it very much.'

He stood up, bent to kiss me gently on the forehead, then walked quickly back to the house.

I sat there on my own in the dark for a while, to think over everything. It had happened so quickly. I'd gone from the depths of despair to the height of joy in less than half an hour. Now I was left with a warm feeling inside, knowing that Glyn loved me, that he really cared.

Beginning to feel chilled in my flimsy mermaid outfit, I rose and made my way back to the house. The party was in full swing now. More guests had arrived and figures in all kinds of weird outfits were jostling each other in every room, in the hall and on the stairs.

I wanted to be with Glyn. Even though I hadn't wanted him to kiss me, I thought we could have spent the rest of the evening together. Then I reminded myself that this was Glyn's party, he had to act as host and mix with everybody.

Entering the room where the music was blaring,

where all the dancing was going on, I looked round to see if I recognized anyone. I noticed Eric's red hair as he danced with someone I didn't know. But all the other faces were unfamiliar.

I decided to go to the kitchen for some more refreshments. Not that I was at all hungry – though the spread that mum had helped prepare was very tempting – but eating and drinking gave me something to do with my hands, so that I felt less awkward among all these strangers.

The kitchen was empty, and most of the food was gone. I helped myself to some fruit salad that remained, then looked around for some orange squash or Coke. All I could see was a bowl of punch which I knew contained some alcohol, so I opened a door that looked as if it led to a larder, hoping there might be some soft drinks inside.

But the door would only open a couple of inches. Something was in the way. There was a stifled giggle – a girl's – then Glyn's voice. 'Go away, we're busy.'

I froze. He'd actually lied about Moira having gone home! They were in here together. Furious, I pushed at the door with all my strength.

'Ouch! Stop it. What do you think you're doing?' cried the girl's indignant voice. Gwen's voice. They both came out, looking rather sheepish. Gwen's scarlet lipstick was smudged and quite a lot of it had transferred itself to Glyn's grinning face.

The grin vanished when he saw me. Then he put it back on again and started talking too quickly.

'Boy, am I glad to see you, Jacky! I hope you've come to rescue me from this scheming minx. Would you believe she forced me in here? No, I don't suppose you would . . .'

Gwen giggled, then stopped as she saw the look on my face.

'I suppose you were saying goodbye to Gwen too.' My voice was shaking with anger. 'You must have thought I was such an idiot.' Not wanting to make an even bigger fool of myself, I ran out of the room.

This time it was Gwen who came after me. I was half-way between Glyn's house and the bungalow when she caught up with me.

'Jacky! I didn't realize you had a thing going with Glyn. Honestly, I had no idea. When we told you about his other holiday romances you didn't seem bothered.'

I stopped and looked at her. Standing there in her St Trinian's outfit, her face was serious, concerned. I remembered what she and John had said about the girl last summer. What had I thought then? I suppose I hadn't believed them, thought they were teasing. But why should they be? They didn't know I cared.

'Well, I didn't mention it because I didn't want anyone to think I was trying to steal him away from Moira,' I explained. Gwen gave me a pitying smile.

'I doubt if anyone would do that, not in the long term. Oh, they're always falling out, always flirting with other people. They're two of a kind. They'll be back together tomorrow, or next week.'

'He told me they've definitely split up.'

'Well, he probably thinks they have. They always think they mean it at the time. But I'm warning you, even if it is over, you've still got a lot of competition.'

'So I gather. But you can cross me off your list of rivals, Gwen. I withdraw!'

With that, I walked on, making it clear our discussion was over. Shrugging, she turned back to the party.

Chapter 18

I stumbled my way along the cliff path in the darkness, away from Glyn's house and the bungalow, away from Glanheli. I didn't know where I was going on my own through the dark and I didn't care. I only knew I didn't want to go back to mum and dad and Mrs Rees in the bungalow, couldn't either attempt to make polite conversation as if nothing had happened, or make a fool of myself by showing them my grief.

My pride was all I had left. In front of Gwen I'd fought to keep my cool, to choke back the tears, but now I was alone they streamed down my face. I'd stood on the back porch of the bungalow trying to think up excuses for leaving the party early, then realizing I couldn't face it, I'd slipped away up the drive and on to the cliff path.

As with swimming, walking briskly helped to ease my feelings. I thought back to the way Glyn had behaved all along and I had to admit to myself that my first impression of him had been right. He *was* big-headed and he *had* only been flirting with me. Nothing he'd done afterwards had – or should have – corrected that impression. He'd wasted no time in trying to charm me while Moira was away. His reluctance to do anything behind her back was only pretended to make me keener, and to give him an opportunity to play around with Gwen. He'd even admittted going out with her, and like a fool I'd accepted they were just friends.

How daft can you get? I'd ignored the evidence of my own eyes, and John's warning. I'd believed what I wanted to believe, that Glyn was in love with me. I remembered the way he'd whispered it in my ear tonight. Charmingly, disarmingly – as though he'd had plenty of practice.

Almost a mile now lay between me and Glyn's house. I paused, turning back to look at the pretty coloured lights decorating the garden, still hearing faint sounds of merrymaking from the house. There are no lonelier sounds than music and laughter when you know you have no part in them.

I began to feel cold, but still walked on, the wind whipping my face and body, my bare arms and shoulders, bending the tall sea-grasses that grew in tufts at the bottom of the cliff. The waves creamed and frothed on the black shore. Moonlight gleamed on the foam, giving it a phosphorescent life of its own.

Once more the sea, and the silly costume I was still wearing, reminded me of Hans Andersen's tale of the mermaid, who would dissolve into foam on the waves if she failed to win the heart of her loved one. Dissolving – that was exactly how I felt.

How could I bear to live at Nant Garregog, go to the same school as Glyn and watch him playing around with other girls?

I shivered. It was really cold now, yet I hated the thought of having to turn back and face everyone. So when I came to a kind of little gully in the cliff, leading down to the beach, I turned into it. Here it was more sheltered. I leaned against a clump of sea-grass and wondered if anyone had missed me yet.

Suddenly I was aware of a shape looming up in front of me, black against the grey, faintly moonlit cliff. A man, coming towards me. Could it be dad – or Glyn – come to look for me? Or was the dark figure that of a stranger, perhaps with some evil purpose?

It couldn't be Glyn. He would have brought Gelert. I began to pray that it was dad. As the figure neared, it seemed its head was unnaturally large, misshapen. Or was it a trick of the dim light?

All the warnings I'd ever been given about wandering in lonely places on my own filled my mind, spurring on my imagination. Was this some sort of malformed monster?

'Jacky, is that you?' I vaguely recognized that quiet, diffident voice. Surely it couldn't be . . .

The black figure removed its deepsea diver's helmet.

'John!' I jumped up and ran to him, sobbing with relief:

'Hey, Jacky, what's the matter? It can't be that

bad!' He looked surprised and embarrassed as I flung my arms round his black rubber suit and hugged him. I was just so pleased it was only him and not some sinister stranger!

'Well, Jacky, I didn't expect this! But I must say it's a nice surprise.'

'What made you come to look for me?'

'I asked Gwen where you were, and she told me what had happened. I went over to your bungalow to see if you were all right, and your parents seemed to think you were still at the party. So I was worried.'

'Did you tell anyone else?'

'No, I thought I'd come and look for you myself first. I remembered you telling me that day in Nant Garregog that you like walking on your own, so I guessed you might have come this way. I'm glad I've found you. It's dangerous on your own at night.'

This was quite a long speech, coming from John. I felt grateful that he'd thought of checking that I was OK. Still standing very close to him, I realized from the look on his face that he was pleased at my nearness.

'Why don't you kiss me, John?'

'I'd love to but I'm shy. Maybe you'd better kiss me.'

I reached up and pulled his face down to mine. Our lips met and his arms encircled me. Before I knew what was happening he'd lifted me off my feet, laid me down on the sandy grass and was covering my face, neck and shoulders with kisses.

'Wow, I thought you were shy!' I gasped.

'You've helped me overcome it,' he murmured,

kissing me again. I found, to my amazement, that I enjoyed it as much as Glyn's kiss. Yet, I'd thought that John didn't attract me.

He stood up and pulled me to my feet. 'Come on, my little mermaid, it's time we were getting back.'

For a while we walked in silence, not touching. I was feeling confused. How could I have reacted like that to John when I was in love with Glyn?

We were a few yards from the house when John spoke, sounding gruff and uncomfortable.

'Were you really so glad to see me, Jacky? Or was it only because you were upset? You never seemed interested before.'

'I don't know. I feel I want you to put your arm round me, hold my hand. But maybe I just want someone to comfort me because Glyn let me down.' I had to be honest. It wouldn't be fair to let him get the wrong idea.

He sighed. 'I was afraid of that. But I want to comfort you, because I like you very much, Jacky.' He put his arms round me and kissed me, gently this time.

'I'll take you home now. And I'll phone you tomorrow, see how you feel.'

Chapter 19

The September sunlight slants into Jubilee Street as I sit at my desk near the bedroom window, writing. It's a different kind of story this time: about what actually happened instead of about things I wished for, but hardly dared to hope. A story about myself, John and Glyn, set in Glanheli – only I've had to change all the names, of course.

What set it off was the letter from *Sweet Sixteen* that was waiting for me when we arrived home. It said I hadn't won the prize, so I shan't be taking anyone off to Italy, or even for a weekend in Scotland. But – and this is the good news – the editor said she liked a lot of things about my story and she thought my writing showed 'promise'. She suggested that I try to write a love story about an ordinary girl of my age, set in a place I really know well, and send it to her. So that's what I'm doing now.

I'm starting at the sixth form in the school Glyn goes to, but it'll be three weeks later than everyone else. We have got to sell our house here, but dad has got his money through now so we've bought the cottages at Nant Garregog. As soon as the tourist season finishes, at the beginning of next month, we can have the bungalow next door to Glyn at a very low rent while the cottages are being done up. Dad's planning to do quite a lot of work there himself.

And by next June, or even Easter if things go well, our café should be in business. June, her husband and the baby will be coming to us in Wales for Christmas. Did I tell you about the baby? A little girl, seven pounds, three ounces. They've called her Amber, would you believe.

She's gorgeous. For the first time, I sort of envied June as she held that tiny, new life in her arms. Mum will be sorry to leave them too, but June will be well enough to cope by the time we move.

They've already begun work on the road down to the Nant. I agree with Glyn, it's a shame about it not being secret any more, but that road got things going for our family.

Glyn. For a few days I was so mad I wouldn't even speak to him. Then I had a long chat with Mrs Rees, and she explained to me how a boy who is an only child without a father can sometimes have difficulty in making relationships with girls.

'He seems to find it all too easy!' I commented.

She laughed. 'I know what you mean. But it's true. A boy in that position has to be careful not to get too close to his mum. He doesn't want to become a "mother's boy", you see. But it becomes a habit not to get too close to anyone. And one way of not getting too close is to play around.'

Thinking of the way Glyn seemed so sincere at times, I realized that's because he was – at the time. But he'll have to solve his problems with someone else, because I'm not going to be fooled again.

After the night of Glyn's party, John phoned me every day, gradually getting quite talkative as he forgot his shyness. Then he took me to see the little castle I'd looked at through my window.

'At least it's real,' I said, 'even if it is a folly.'

'Some of your castles have got to be real,' was John's mysterious reply. I'd told him all about my 'castles in the fire'. Those castles representing my hopes and dreams for the future. I think he was trying to say the same thing as Mrs Rees. Some daydreams are just mirages that crumble into dust when you get near them, but others keep on taking definite form until they eventually become solid.

Some dreams come true. But you never know which ones.

heartlines

Where true love comes first

Other books in the series for you to enjoy

Anita Davies
Stepsisters £1.25

Ross was the most exciting thing that had ever happened to Laurie. She hadn't expected to enjoy the party much, but as soon as she entered the kitchen, she'd seen his dark eyes smouldering at her. He was gorgeous, and, at twenty, much more mature than Peter. After a walk in the moonlight with Ross, nothing could be further from her mind than those all-important 'O' Levels.

But trouble loomed – homework was left undone, her dreams of finding the ideal stepsister had ended disastrously in a bitter row with her best friend, and worst of all, her mother had banned her from going out on Saturday. And that meant she couldn't see Ross . . .

Ann Ruffell
Leaving Home £1.50

DOES ABSENCE MAKE THE HEART GROW FONDER?

"It's time you left home and learned to live on your own," Sue's parents decided. And when her best friend Judy started talking about their moving into a flat together, she began to dream of independence.

It seemed idyllic until Sue's boyfriend Mike went off to college. Then she spent her nights writing him long and romantic letters, dreaming of the time when she'd see him again. Or she did until Paul came round. He was funny, friendly and a good listener. Mike seemed very far away . . .

Jane Butterworth
Born to be Wild £1.99

How dare he tell us how to run our lives when we were happy? If I ever set eyes on him again, I'd tell him to go back to his stupid Marietta!

Jossy had spent all her life in the commune. Secluded from the outside world in the depths of rural Wales, it had become a haven of peace for her family and their friends.

Then Alex arrives, on holiday with his parents. At first, Jossy is repelled by his trendy London ways. But then her feelings for him grow, feelings that threaten to challenge her life, her hopes, and everything she believes in . . .

Spotlight on Sam £1.25

Sam was always putting herself down. She was too tall, her nose too long, her feet too big, and she wasn't much good at anything. Things look better though, when her natural talent for the stage lands her with a part – and a date from Tom, the dishy assistant stage manager.

All Pan books are available at your local bookshop or newsagent, or can be ordered direct from the publisher. Indicate the number of copies required and fill in the form below.

Send to: CS Department, Pan Books Ltd., P.O. Box 40,
             Basingstoke, Hants.   RG21 2YT.

or phone: 0256 469551 (Ansaphone), quoting title, author
             and Credit Card number.

Please enclose a remittance* to the value of the cover price plus: 60p for the first book plus 30p per copy for each additional book ordered to a maximum charge of £2.40 to cover postage and packing.

*Payment may be made in sterling by UK personal cheque, postal order, sterling draft or international money order, made payable to Pan Books Ltd.

Alternatively by Barclaycard/Access:

Card No. | | | | | | | | | | | | | | | | |

Signature:

Applicable only in the UK and Republic of Ireland.

While every effort is made to keep prices low, it is sometimes necessary to increase prices at short notice. Pan Books reserve the right to show on covers and charge new retail prices which may differ from those advertised in the text or elsewhere.

NAME AND ADDRESS IN BLOCK LETTERS PLEASE:

....

Name ————————————————————————————————

Address ——————————————————————————————

————————————————————————————————————

————————————————————————————————————

————————————————————————————————————

3/87